ON THE PUNISHMENT OF DEATH.

FRANÇOIS GUIZOT

FV EDITIONS

CONTENTS

PREFACE.

It may be asked, perhaps, what I hope from this work? I do not hope, I admit, that governments will be convinced of the inutility of capital punishment, still less that they will abandon its employment. Truth glides slowly into the mind of power, and even when it does fairly enter, it is not immediately acknowledged as master. The mind long refuses to believe, and even when forced to believe, it still refuses to obey. There is no occasion to tell why.

It is precisely for this reason, that when power is in error, it is necessary to set the public right—to establish in opinion that which will be so long of resolving into fact. If the road is long, it is the more necessary to set out early; for in that case, even before reaching the goal, we may obtain some results. It is vain to prolong error, for when known to be such, it is powerless. Society in the present day is so formed, that power is half vanquished when the public pronounces it to be in the wrong. In vain it persists, for even in persisting, it hesitates, feeling itself to be before a superior strength. Opinion at length gradually comes to invade, where before it only sustained attack; but even then power does not yield, though its hesitation increases. First fear, and then doubt, weakens its action: then it becomes timid, and falls into the mistake of employing a means which society reprobates, and in the efficacy of which it does not itself believe. To this point it must be forced, and its errors clearly exhibited; and at last, as the daylight shines upon them, the strength in which it trusted will be more difficult to use, and be more and more weakened by the increasing blunders of its strategy.

I think the present time favourable for thus attacking the use of capital punishment in the light of a political question. When action is directed by truth, it is slow and feeble; but it proceeds vigorously when truth works in the way of reaction. Amid the gentle manners of the eighteenth century, cruel laws, political severities, and the punishment of death, were vigorously striven against: everything seemed tending to restrain, if not suppress them, and many honest men supposed the victory gained. But the Revolution broke out, and cruel laws, political severity, and the punishment of death, were resorted to with a violence unheard of before. So many perished hopes engendered a fear that the ideas which had given them birth were an illusion; but this was a great error. On the contrary, it is at this time that these ideas may claim and exercise the greatest dominion; they are able to avail themselves of a recent and frightful experience; and it is easy for them, in improving it, to rid themselves of the dreams of their infancy, to strengthen themselves by instances instead of theories, and to come down to the simplest rules of common sense.

Notwithstanding the scepticism of our time, the public mind is disposed to receive them. The Revolution made more enemies by employing capital punishment politically, than were stirred up by all the books and speeches philanthropic, philosophical, and literary. It has left on this subject an impression much more efficacious than that of ideas, and which overcomes opinions even the most apparently hostile. With many men it would provoke indignation to try to make them admit even the partial suppression of capital punishment as a general necessity, the consequences of a right or a theory: perhaps they would say that it is such chimeras which brought on the Revolution. But place these same men in the presence of facts: let them award, in the capacity of judges or juries, the terrible sentence, or even let them see it brought into effect by others, and experience will resume all its power over their minds. They will mistrust its necessity and its justice; melancholy presentiments will arise from melancholy recollections; they will feel at once doubt and fear; they will recall what they have seen, and what they have suffered; they will distrust a policy which has occasion to take such a course, and engenders such a necessity; and they will have no more faith in results than in reasons. And thus in spite of theoretical opinions, often in spite even of the tendency of circumstances, the common instinct, the public good sense—fruit of bitter experience—will resist the employment of capital punishment politically with much more efficacy than all the arguments and precepts of philosophy.

I would justify this instinct, and produce all the proofs of its legitimacy. Is the case urgent? Does power show itself so eager for, and so prodigal of, capital punishment? Are we so assailed by penalties that it is necessary to sound the alarm, and to treat the policy of our days as if it resembled that disastrous policy the severe judgments of which were formerly its great and habitual instruments? I detest exaggeration, for it is falsehood. I do not seek to excite or maintain blind fears of what I cannot prove; I draw no comparison between our own and those deplorable times. But let me not be told that it is necessary to wait in a case like this for the right to speak. If the punishment of death is politically useless, inefficacious, and even dangerous, wherefore not say so at once? Why should truth be silent till it is proclaimed by facts so terrible? These facts, it may be said, will not come: well, if they are not to come, a book cannot bring them; and if they are, who could pardon himself if he had delayed the warning? Besides, I observe the odd anomaly, that some people, when afraid, are at once credulous and difficult of belief. Sometimes they see frightful symptoms everywhere; and sometimes they will not believe in the possibility of the evil till its arrival. One would say that they made a choice in their recollections; always accessible to some, and repulsing others as importunate and inadmissible.

The least idea, the slightest agitation, recalls the terrors of the Revolution to their minds; but with other terrors before them, likewise revolutionary, they are blind and bold. They are seized with affright if some errors of the Constituent Assembly reappear, and yet exclaim against any inquietude that may be manifested on the restoration of capital punishment as a political engine. I ask more impartiality of memory, more extent in foresight, and more justice in fear. We are not descended so low that an evil must be horrible to be felt. I am sure that iniquity without modesty and without restraint has not taken possession of either the laws or tribunals; I know that if it aspired too far, it would meet with powerful obstacles in its course; and I am aware that danger does not lurk at every door, or the punishment of death hover over all the adversaries of power. But still, in my opinion, capital punishment is too often called for, and too often inflicted. In the use we make of it there is neither wisdom, nor equity, nor necessity; it fails in its object, and aggravates the evil of our position by engaging power in a course full of peril for society and for itself; it causes of itself gratuitous misfortunes, which, if they spread no farther, are still neither lighter nor more reparable; it attaches itself to a false and fatal policy, and sinks day by day into an instrument more melancholy and more useless. Let others imagine that there are not here sufficient motives for opposing its use, and wait for more evils and more severity: for my part I think I have reckoned enough.

Another consideration determines me. One side has triumphed, and expecting still to triumph, it in the meantime does all it can. It will attempt, I think, more than it has yet attempted; although it cannot do all it would. This is evident even to itself. The situation is a new one. In the course of the Revolution, the party which succeeded always did more than it intended, and more than at the commencement of the enterprise it was in a condition even to conceive. The success surpassed not only hopes, but pretensions. Blind instruments of a giant power, the men of the Revolution were hurried away by events more rapid than their thoughts, and carried facts into accomplishment much more extensive and terrible than their designs.

Now, on the contrary, we see a party in authority whose desires surpass their designs, and whose designs surpass their power. They would advance, and they do so; but at each step their hope lessens of attaining their end. Instead of being, like the Revolutionists, carried onwards by their momentum rather than their will, they are held back against their will by a force contrary to their momentum.

With nothing, or almost nothing active and visible to oppose them, everything around is resistance; everything troubles and delays them —the instruments they employ, the air which surrounds them, the ground which they tread beneath their feet.

Whence arises this anomaly, and what does it reveal to us of the fate of the party? I do not care to busy myself with this question. I merely remark the general fact, and I do so because it has consequences of which I wish to avail myself.

It is in such moments that the truth is good to be told, although it will not be the better received by men to whom it is displeasing, or exercise more power over great events. No party disavows its origin, none acquires that high wisdom which, in changing its nature, would change its whole destiny; even if the progress it is able to make in skill or prudence is not sufficiently extended, or prompt to save them from that definitive fate to which Providence has devoted them. These parties are no more independent than other things of the action of time. Their internal dispositions become modified as well as their situation, and these modifications render them more or less accessible to the influence of truth. When a party is carried away by the general movement of the age, when it becomes the engine of a great social crisis, neither truth nor wisdom has any effect upon its career. It crushes all who oppose it, abandons all who counsel it, and hurries blindly onwards to a goal of which it is ignorant; and it is then that, in the midst of their greatest activity, we see most clearly the weakness of men—the mere tools in working out decrees alike beyond their understanding and their will. But when the social tempest is calmed, and Providence seems to have given up the management of human affairs to ordinary laws, and the contending parties have time to look around them, to study their course, and to measure their strength, we see them resume some reason with their freedom. Instead of the fever which devoured them, a new malady gains upon them, a slow and heavy dissolution, which, without destroying the predominant character or general intentions of the party, gives more independence to individuals, and more authority to wisdom. In the course of the Revolution, the partisans of monarchy detached themselves from the Constituents, the Constituents from the Girondins, and the Girondins from the

Jacobins; but the Revolution, far from being stopped or slackened, pursued with even more violence its terrible career; and in proportion as these factions became wiser, they became less powerful.

Who would think now-a-days that any one of the parties into which we are divided could thus deliver itself up to the madness of its wishes and passions, denouncing and trampling whoever refused to cooperate, and that yet it would gain strength every day, and march rapidly towards success? Nothing like this can now be seen. If in these parties there be any one who still hopes to the contrary, he is a dreamer blind to passing events, and who has neither forgotten nor learnt. Whether conquerors or beaten, outs or ins, all parties are constrained to act with wisdom and prudence: the energy of fever will not now suffice for strength; they must rally around their banner all shades of interests or opinions; for they cannot suffer one to fall away without feeling instantly its loss in their own weakness. They must even bend in some measure before their more obstinate adversaries; and this is not a counsel I give, but a fact I observe, and one which in every day more apparent in their conduct.

It is seen clearly in the party now in power, and under two characters: there is a division in the party, and in a contrary direction to that which took place twenty-nine years ago. It is not the most violent, but the most moderate and prudent, who now take the management of its affairs—those who have the best chance of enlisting general interests and floating opinions.

Even these moderates are evidently driven farther than they desire, and perhaps may end in being overturned. But in their case they will not be replaced by the more violent; the party will drag itself from impotence to impotence, just as revolution is precipitated from fury to fury. And after the evil they have caused—the greatest evil in their power—dissolved by their success, as well as weakened by their old reverses, they will be forced to feel that they have undertaken an impossibility, and that no one in the present day is able to bring about a revolution in society.

Things being in this position, it may be advantageous to throw into the midst of parties what appears to me to be the truth. No one is more aware than myself that they will not make it their rule, but it will operate as a dissolvent, insinuating itself into their disorganised constitution. It will not be met by those proud convictions, that blind confidence, that idea of an ardent and insurmountable force, which prevented its access to the revolutionary parties. The party which predominates at the present day is full of doubt and fear; it has faith neither in its own doctrines nor its own destiny. In assuming to be the protector of order, it sometimes tries to appropriate the principles of liberty. Whether it courts them because it feels its own to be decayed, or merely as a mask, is of little consequence; what is certain is, that it is surrounded by obstacles, obliged to adopt the means of government it distrusts, to speak in a language which scandalises a portion of its adherents, to temporise, and to hesitate—and all these things open a way for truth, and give it opportunity as it advances to second the uncertainty, internal feebleness, and moral dissolution by which the party is beset. A simple fact will demonstrate this: in 1791 and 1792 the opposition in its harangues only served to irritate and accelerate the party which accomplished the Revolution. Now the opposition is not less displeasing to the governing party; but it startles it by a word, calms, obliges it to dissemble, and carries confusion into its proceedings and hesitation into its projects. It even enlightens the whole changing mass, insinuates ideas into its bosom, and necessitates a prudence before unthought of, and at which it grumbles and submits. Opposition, then, is not vain; it may have at the present moment few visible or direct effects, but it is at least able to sow, and the future will reap the fruits.

Such are the motives which impel me to write, and I believe them to be sufficient and well-founded.

LIMITS OF THE QUESTION.

It is not a philosophical question of which I wish to treat, neither do I solicit a change in legislation. This is not a time at once calm and active enough for the principles and reformation of the laws to be discussed: but prudence is necessary at all times; and at all times, whatever may be its perils, government may commit useless faults, and cause superfluous evils to society. It is in this point of view that I wish to consider capital punishment as a political question. I would know whether the government, which has the power of prosecuting and pardoning, acts wisely when it has recourse to it, whether it consults its own interest in doing so, and whether it is constrained thereto by necessity.

It will be admitted that this is still worth the trouble of examination. Conspiracies crowd upon us. One has just been brought under judgment at Tours, another at Marseilles, and another at Nantes; the same thing is to be done at Colmar, Rochelle, and Saumur; and if we may believe the authorities which have discovered them, there are many others ready for the law. Sirejean and Vallé have been executed. New condemnations, perhaps new executions, are preparing. If they should prove useless, nay, fatal to the power which commands them!—a mistake here would surely be a melancholy one: if we take life, we should at least be convinced of the necessity for doing so.

Let those who think there is no mistake, be not too hasty in saying so. I affirm that they do themselves doubt, and that without ceasing to think they must continue to doubt. The time has been when, in a struggle among factions, or between them and the governing power, the punishment of death was not only the habitual arm, but a recognised necessity of the conqueror. It is not from seeing this punishment written in the old laws that we know the impression it made upon men, for it is also written in ours; but it had then more foundation in the manners of the time.

The justice of its application was sometimes questioned, but never its utility. Power made use of it with confidence, and none were shocked by the fact. Condemnations and executions might agonize the friends of the vanquished; but the iniquity of such steps not being evident to the public, they considered them as only natural; and power in taking them, firmly believed that it was merely exercising its right, and obeying the necessity of its situation. It was thought by all that government and established order could not be maintained but by the physical destruction of its enemies.

If we now examine the government and the public when capital punishment has been pronounced, or when an execution has just taken place, or is about to do so—if we listen to words, examine thoughts, and interrogate countenances, we shall find everywhere doubt and anxiety. Power has prosecuted: was it right in provoking this judgment? It has struck: has it proved its strength or increased its peril? It does not know itself what to think: it hesitates, and almost apologises for what has been done. And this is not from the fear of appearing cruel, but because it is not sure of having been, I will not say just, but wise. It sought security, and found fear. Thus all its proceedings on such occasions are full of irresolution and inconsistency. A political prosecution pressed forward to-day is held back tomorrow; now it will try to extend its meshes, and anon to contract them; the smallest respite, an application for pardon from the meanest prisoner who has been condemned, becomes an important affair, which calls for long deliberations, the responsibility of which is thought to be of fearful importance; and neither the ill success of the conspiracy, nor the firmest credit in the Chambers, can reassure power from feeling the inquietude which besets it when obliged to accomplish an act it declares to be necessary.

The same impression is made upon the public, which, however, is less moved, since it has nothing to decide. I do not speak of those men who, without conspiring or acting against the government, bear ill-will against it, or even of those whose habits of constitutional opposition render them suspicious of the acts and intentions of power. I address myself to that immense public who have neither political passions nor prejudices, but who desire the establishment of legal order and liberty, because these are necessary for their own wellbeing, for their business, and their daily interests. Are they inclined to imagine it justice which condemns a man to death for a political offence? Do they promise themselves more order and repose after such a consummation! Do they suppose this rigour wholesome, and does it appear necessary to their common sense?

No: it startles them like a disorder, and they do not admit its urgency, or perhaps even its equity. It is difficult to persuade them that power is under any necessity of killing a man; and if there is a necessity, they will perhaps infer that the power itself must be evil. This proceeds neither from a bad feeling against authority, nor from effeminacy of manners, but solely from an unconscious but deep-rooted doubt of the usefulness as well as justice of the punishment. There is scarcely any person in our day out of the pale of faction who, after a political execution, believes the public peace more secure, or the government itself more firmly established; everybody, on the contrary, has less confidence in the strength of power, and in the future of society; and this is not by reason of the conspiracies, but of their punishment. This feeling does not surprise me, for I think it well-founded, and I shall proceed to state why. The government strikes, and the people behold the stroke, but neither the one nor the other is assured after the blow of having gained anything by it.

I have said enough, I think, to prove that there is here matter for debate. I do not suppose that government wishes to make a habit of killing only because this was done formerly, or that it acts solely to please its own passions, and satisfy its own vengeance. The use of the scaffold cannot become a mere routine; and as to the passions which it is pretended have something to say in it, I leave them out of the question, not only because they are not just, but because they are not true. It is not true that they are so strong, so persevering, and so imperious as they are made to appear. If, after having long suffered, they had sacrificed much; if they had refused themselves the consolations of life and the pleasures of the world; if they had shown themselves inflexible and incurable, nourishing in solitude their melancholy and their hope, I could comprehend, perhaps even excuse, their exigence. But they can be easily turned aside, or made to smile; and their violence has not been able to resist either the continuation of danger or the hope of security. As they do not, then, demand a satisfaction they are so well able to dispense with, they have not the right to appear ardent and severe. Such energy comes too late; and since they have no pretensions to depth, they may at least leave us the advantage of their frivolity.

Neither have I anything to question with the laws. They pronounce the punishment of death against political crime, yet I repeat that I do not blame them, that I do not invoke their abolition. I am convinced that the reforms solicited by the sentiments and manners of the time must pass into the conduct of the government, in the routine of its affairs, before being introduced into legislation. So it may be in this matter.

Government influences the prosecution of political crimes; it can often stifle them before they grow of sufficient importance to come before the tribunals; it may invest them with more or less gravity; and finally, it has the right of suspending or mitigating the punishments which the law decrees. Is it necessary for it to provoke the application of capital punishment, or to allow it to be inflicted? That is my whole question. The doubt exists in every mind, even in that of the government itself; and for my part I think the doubt is in the right.

2

PHYSICAL EFFICACY OF CAPITAL PUNISHMENT.

The necessity of punishments depends upon their efficacy. If a punishment does not attain the end proposed in inflicting it, there can be no question that it is unnecessary.

The efficacy of punishments is either physical, or moral, or both. It is physical by the impotence to which it reduces the guilty, and moral by the example it offers. The physical efficacy of the punishment of death was at first its most powerful recommendation. In killing an enemy, it did away with danger; and what could be more natural than to gratify vengeance while insuring safety?

In the present day, however, there is no longer any question of revenge. No legislation, no government, wishes to have imputed to it such barbarity. But every society and every government still desires security; and capital punishment seems to offer it.

But the efficacy of punishments is not the same in all places or at all times. It varies according to the different stages of society, the degrees of civilisation, the sentiments of the people, and the circumstances of government. Capital punishment, in spite of appearances, has not, even in a physical sense, the advantage of an immutable efficacy; for in suppressing a known enemy, it does not always suppress danger.

What was formerly the composition of society? A small aristocracy, rich and powerful; and the multitude poor, obscure, and weak, notwithstanding numerical strength. When a conspiracy was hatched by the great, it had its known and important chiefs, invested with immense power: it was the fruit of the ambition of some men, perhaps only of one, and the work of a few personal influences. On seizing two or three of the conspirators, therefore, the danger was over.

The Percy family, after having placed Henry Lancaster on the throne of England, becoming discontented, conspired and made war against him; but they were defeated and proscribed, and Henry had nothing more to dread. Where are now those eminent and avowed chiefs, whom to destroy was to destroy a party? Under what proper names are peril and influence thus concentrated! Few men now-a-days have a name, and these few are of little consequence. Power has departed from individuals and families; it has left the hearths where it formerly dwelt, to spread itself abroad in society. There it circulates rapidly, and though scarcely seen in any particular spot, it is present everywhere. It is attached to the public interests, ideas, and sentiments, which no single person directs, which no one represents in such a manner as to make their fate depend in the slightest degree upon his. But if these forces are hostile to power, let it search and inquire in what hands they are deposited. Upon what head will it let fall its vengeance? There are still reformers and leaguers, but no longer a Coligny or a Mayenne. The death of an enemy is now but that of a man, and neither troubles nor weakens the party he served. If power is reassured when the life is taken, it deceives itself: its danger remains the same, for it was not the man who created it. The causes of its perils are widely-scattered and deeply-seated; and the absence of a nominal chief does not lessen their energy, or even modify their action. They do not need interpreters, instruments, or councils. The interests and opinions now exist on their own account, and are directed by their own prudence, and make their way by their own strength. No one has a monopoly of them, and no one can either lose them by mischance or sell them by treachery.

Capital punishment, in this at least, has lost its efficacy: it has no longer the prompt and sure result of taking off the head to which all eyes are directed, or of silencing the voice which speaks to all. It may search among these higher classes, in which it is said are the chiefs of parties; but whatever individual it may fix upon, in destroying him, it by no means neutralises the impending danger.

Have governments any instinctive knowledge of this fact? Does it exercise even unconsciously an influence over their conduct? One is tempted to believe so. During the last seven years, many conspiracies in France have been prosecuted and punished; but no man of consideration or of known name had a part in them. Was this because power did not fear such men, or because it thought it could gain little by ridding itself of them? Yet it affirms constantly that every faction has its chiefs, wealthy and important men, who direct its motions and defray its expenses. How is it that these chiefs always escape detection, or that they are reserved for the parade of the tribune, but omitted in the actions before the tribunals?

The true cause is this, and it is of importance to remark it, because it proves my assertion—that the Revolution has struck down in a special manner the upper classes. I use this word the rather because it was the class, not the individual, it was the object of the Revolution to strike. Destined to change society, it was not against men, but against interests and positions, that it directed its blows. The horrible spectacle of judicial death has made so deep an impression, that great hesitation is felt in reviving its use in these more elevated regions. Desires have been expressed, intentions half revealed, even attempts begun; but as soon as any point has been reached from which, if entered, there would be no return, the courage, the will, and the capacity to do have been at an end. At this point the counsels of power are divided; its agents are timid, and its partisans refuse their support. They feel instinctively—and not less wisely—that they are entering on a frightful path, without reason to guide or profit to reward them. To treat the classes that have made the Revolution in the same manner as the Revolution has treated those it has vanquished—to act against it as it has acted against its enemies—is impossible; the very thought is madness. Why, then, direct such fury against individuals whose death would be attended with more noise than benefit? Why recommence in the bosom of the higher class that bloody struggle which will serve to excite hatred against power without really weakening its enemies? Is it necessary again to let the people see that neither consideration, fortune, nor elevated station, is any protection against the violence of political passions? They have begun to forget this, and become accustomed to believe that there are social conditions which, from their nature, are strangers to tumult and its consequences, and where the punishment of death almost never penetrates. Should this salutary belief be broken down? Should the multitude be taught that there are conspiracies in those ranks which are the most interested in maintaining order, and the exhibition presented to them of a man well-known, influential, and highly esteemed, dragged to the scaffold like the vilest malefactor? Might not more danger accrue from this spectacle than from the most powerful adversary of government? Is it not by such spectacles that the Revolution overturned not only society, but habits and ideas? Besides, when such a war takes place among men of the same position, education, and rank, it wears a much more serious aspect than elsewhere: the combatants have known, seen, and spoken to each other; those who are defeated know by whom they are so, by whom their destruction has been sought; and their friends will remember it to-morrow: thus enmities become personal, and dangers direct. Is it prudent or is it unavoidable to allow the strife to assume this character?

Will men compromise themselves in person, when even success cannot avert danger, for the simple reason that danger lies in many more things than the life or hostility of individuals? Thus in proportion as the chiefs of a party become less important, the more hesitation is felt in destroying them; and the fear of incurring such responsibility is not surmounted by any feeling of its imperious necessity. That spontaneous good sense which directs men almost unconsciously, informs the friends and even depositaries of power that they would have to hunt after the life of their principal adversaries with less profit to their cause than peril to themselves. Three centuries ago, the destruction of a known enemy was our grand object; now such a consummation is dreaded and shunned: and notwithstanding the fierce declarations and blind fury of certain agents, notwithstanding even its own passions, when government is able and ready to strike the enemies it professes to fear, it surrounds itself with a coil of circumstances to prevent the blow, which compromises without serving.

It is said that men are cowardly, each seeking his own safety, and unwilling to put himself forward on behalf of the government. All that may be true; but if there was any necessity in the case, if the strength or safety of power centered in the destruction of certain men, there would not be wanting friends or agents to hire out their courage to their ambition or their servility. But even the vices of human nature change their mode of action with the time: egotism, covetousness, and fear, do not always follow the same course. No one is a stranger to the new stage of society in which we live, no one is ignorant of the real chiefs of party; the men dangerous in themselves have disappeared, and no one believes that the suppression of such and such an adversary could dissipate, or even sensibly diminish, the dangers of power. The physical inefficacy of capital punishment in the higher ranks is deep in the minds of all. In vain would government refuse its belief, for it is no longer in a condition to act as if it did not believe, and neither fear nor passion has the power of recalling a necessity which no longer exists.

Is the punishment of death more efficacious, and therefore more necessary, against the dangers which spring up lower in society? While the high aristocracy is extinct, and conspiracies are no longer the offspring of a few eminent men, the mass of the free and active population has increased in volume, and exercises an influence it did not formerly possess. Perhaps capital punishment, useless against the fallen great, may be more necessary against the intrigues which ferment in the bosom of the multitude.

I request that it be not forgotten that the necessity of punishment depends upon its efficacy, and likewise that I am now treating of capital punishment only in its physical effects.

And first, I object to the very word **multitude**; that is to say, in the extensive meaning which some persons would give it. To see the insolence with which such persons treat a great population, one would think that we are still in the thirteenth century; that the feudal aristocracy is now in its pride of place; and that it looks down haughtily from the height of its towers on bands of serfs scattered over its domains, or trembling bourgeois coming humbly to solicit permission to rebuild the walls of their poor town, as a defence against robbers. These persons are mistaken: society is not thus formed; there is no longer an abyss separating the higher classes from the mass of the people. The descent from the summit of the social order to its base is by means of close steps, covered with men only slightly different from those above and beneath them. This is true as regards property, industry, education, knowledge, and influence; and although some momentary confusion may be occasioned by the ruins of the old regime, the new form of society is fixed for ever in France. It is necessary to keep this in view, in order to comprehend the effects of legislation and the acts of power, since it is not for the age of Philip-Augustus, but for our own, that we have a government and laws. But let us see how things were managed formerly in the event of political crimes occurring out of the upper region of society, and in what way the governing power proceeded.

On the part of the people plots were rare—the aristocracy had that privilege. This is easily conceivable; for the latter alone could gain by or succeed in them. How could the citizens or peasants conceive the idea of changing the government and seizing the authority? When plots were on foot, they marched in the train of the great, either compelled or seduced. Neither the initiative, nor the direction, nor the fortunate chances of such enterprises, belonged to them.

However, they sometimes troubled the established order. This was by seditions, and general or local revolts, according to the causes which created them—whether oppression, famine, or occasionally new religious creeds. Then the insurrections were frightful: a frenzied multitude quitted their wretched homes, and wandered about in bands, killing, pillaging, and devastating—brutalised in their passions, blind and implacable in their vengeance, ferocious and licentious in their freedom. Such was the war of the peasants of Suabia in Germany, the insurrection of Wat Tyler in England, the Jacquerie in France, and everywhere, from age to age, a crowd of similar risings, less important, but not less hideous.

When such disorders could be repressed before they were converted into wars, it was done without much art. Almost all those who had exerted or seconded them were condemned and executed.

All that was to be done was simply to hunt a population from its soil, setting fire to a score of villages, and covering the roads with bodies or limbs hanging from gibbets.

When the war had broken out, it became a ferocious chase, which terminated only with the death of the insurgents; or if it was thought prudent to treat with and disperse them by promises, the promises disappeared with the bands which had received them. Thus the peril over, even the British parliament supplicated Richard II. not to pay any attention to such pretended concessions, but to give to all his sheriffs and judges full powers to proceed against the rebels on their return to their provinces. It was not alone during the feudal servitude, in the midst of the darkness and barbarism of the middle ages, that popular movements were thus repressed. When order commenced, when the police, military force, and all the rights of sovereignty, were concentrated in the hands of government, the same means were used, but with more regularity. The number of executions which took place in the reign of Henry VIII. was above 70,000, and under Elizabeth still upwards of 19,000, and insurrections and riots did not furnish the smallest part of them. Madame Sévigné informs us in her letters how Louis XIV. punished the trifling seditions of Brittany. 'The whole of the inhabitants of a large street,' she says, 'have been hunted out and banished, and everybody forbidden on pain of death to harbour them; so that all these wretches, women newly delivered, old men and infants, are wandering away weeping from the town, without knowing whither to go, without food, and without a place to lay their heads. ... Sixty citizens have been taken, and are to be hung to-morrow. ... We are no longer so extravagant: one in eight days is now sufficient to keep justice going; and the gallows appears quite a refreshment.' Society did not see all this blood flow, and the king was not aware of all the executions which took place; but that the punishment of death was efficacious in a time in which such things could pass without the knowledge of society or of the king—in a time in which wholesale banishment, the gallows, and the wheel, were not merely punishments, but the ordinary arms of police—surely one must be hard of belief to doubt it. Whether in the thirteenth century, or even later, these means might have been necessary, I will not inquire. What I

know is, that they were possible, and, moreover, that they were physically efficacious, since they really banished in a great measure the
danger against which they were directed, positively reducing the
number and strength of their enemies; falling upon the popular
masses like hail upon a field of corn, cutting off all the petty chiefs,
decimating the fighting-men, and, in fact, not only operating by fear,
but by real enervation.

Could this be done in our day? Would the punishment of death
thus employed have the same efficacy? To those who think so, and at
the same time understand what they think, I have nothing to say,
except that I do not fear them. The system they call for will not have
even the shame of a useless trial. But how many people still believe
in the efficacy of capital punishment, even in its physical point of
view, without taking account of its effects or the tendency of their
own opinion! The remembrance of past times governs their ideas.
Some minds can accommodate themselves at once to the changes of
social order, or even anticipate them; but the greater number
remain blind and motionless long after the consummation has taken
place. The world is full of habits without foundation, and beliefs
without motive. This is an instance of the fact.

What government would now dare to use the punishment of
death against the people in a manner which would render it physically efficacious? and what laws, what ministers, would prescribe or
permit the gallows to be raised along the roads, or shoot men by
hundreds, or dispossess and chase away the inhabitants of a canton?
We are told of the softness of our manners, and the humanity of
our laws; but there are many other obstacles, or rather those sentiments which protect among us the life of a man are themselves
protected by the powerful facts which gave them birth. If human life
is now more respected, it is that it has more force to make itself
respected. Of what consequence was one of the people, a peasant
or a petty bourgeois, in the times when such classes were treated in
the manner we have seen? A miserable being, totally unknown,
weaker and more isolated than the meanest shrub languishing in a
forest of oaks. His views extended no farther than his subsistence;
his death was of as little importance as his life; and the evils of his
lot were as unknown as himself. His fate was allied to nothing; and

no one who held any place in society thought himself compromised by the misfortunes and hardships of the multitude. For that multitude there were distinct laws and particular punishments, from which the higher classes had nothing to fear; and the condemnation and execution of a hundred seditious peasants might take place in the district, without the details being known at a distance of thirty leagues, and without the really influential and active part of the nation feeling the least fear for themselves.

There is not a single man now in this condition in society, not a single being whoso life is of so little moment, and whose execution would make so little noise. It might have been a tempting idea to destroy one's enemies while thus isolated, silent, and obscure; at the slightest insurrection or danger the punishment of death might easily descend upon this humble race, and make havoc among them at its leisure. But now there are fewer great lords and many more men, and these all hold together.

None is so high that the lowest voice cannot reach him; none so strong that the dangers of the weakest may not also threaten him; none so obscure that misfortune may not give importance to his fate; and none so isolated, whether by greatness or insignificance, that he has nothing to hope or fear from what passes around him. The condition of men in society bears now some analogy with the laws of their destiny in the world; there are no invincible inequalities and no privileges; the trials or blessings of Providence are for all; no one is sheltered more than another from misfortune, sickness, or grief; and each sees in the fate of his neighbour the image or presentiment of his own. This community of position, this parity of chances, this equality in the hand of God, is not the least powerful bond of union among men. It attracts them to each other, intermingles them in the same sentiments, hinders them from being kept aloof by the clashing of their interests and the diversity of their conditions; and, in fine, gathers them together under equal laws, and makes them feel that they have one nature and one country. This is the terrestrial destiny of man; and the present state of society begins to shape in the same fashion its political destiny. The same laws and the same chances are given to all; great diversities grow weaker, and community of interest stronger and more

extended. Everything tends to teach men that they are accessible to
the same evils, and exposed to the same perils, and that therefore
they cannot remain indifferent to the fate of each other; while
everything furnishes them with the means of communicating with,
and sustaining each other. Thus, on the one hand, individual existence has more importance and power; and, on the other, the
totality of existence is so closely interlaced and dovetailed, that a
wound or a threat is felt simultaneously, and the means of protection simultaneously adopted.

If we would form an idea of the prodigious changes which, in
the point of view I have taken, this new state of things has introduced into the relations between society and the government, let us
consider what would become of power if it had now to repress in
the people one of those insurrections which formerly it was so easy
to manage by means of the gallows or the wheel. When we see a
crowd in movement, when here and there some cries are heard, and
some cudgels raised, we fancy the state in danger, call out the troops,
and display the public force in its gravest aspect. I do not say that
this is wrong; but what if a province rose, if armed bands traversed
the country, sometimes victorious, and sometimes difficult to
vanquish? This, however, is just what happened under Louis XIV. in
Brittany, Languedoc, and twenty other places: here on account of a
tax, there for a creed, elsewhere against an edict. Troops were sent
out, punishments multiplied, the population hunted; but the confusion had no effect upon the fêtes at Versailles, and the ordinary
course of affairs at Paris was undisturbed; for the state did not feel
itself compromised, or power really attacked.

And wherefore, it will be asked, should these violent resistances
and partial disorders now inspire so much more alarm than
formerly? Is it that they have a more serious effect? It is that they are
no longer a mere effervescence of the multitude; that instead of
popular seditions, there would now be public movements. Such is
the composition of society, that the rabble, reduced in number and
force, can no longer act alone in the brutality of their wants or
passions. Between them and power is placed a great, wealthy, and
yet working population, who, though still too little educated, are
able to see far beyond mere material necessities or the fancies of the

moment. This population is not given to tumults, for its members do not live upon daily wages, but work upon whatever they possess, land or capital. Thus it is very difficult to draw them away from their business; even when discontented, they would long hesitate before acting, for no one has the power to command them; and however bad a government might be, it could scarcely drive them to do worse than grumble. But if an insurrection were really to take place, it could not be without their concurrence and consent. And thus those who, in the seventeenth century, scarcely attracted the attention of Louis XIV. at all, would now set the whole government astir, and cause it to feel that this was no question of a riot among the populace, but that a more formidable enemy and a greater danger were before it. If force was not at once successful, the authorities would despair of force, and have recourse to promises, concessions, changes of systems, to all that compulsory policy which proclaims that power has been mistaken, and has found it out. And thus, while formerly a government, opposing nothing but troops or punishments to the seditious, might be for some years at war with a portion of the country, society, in its quiet, but strong construction, animated by one common spirit, would hardly have advanced a step in real resistance before its tottering government would begin to think rather of reforms than punishments.

Is it then, I ask, is it in the midst of society thus constituted that the physical efficacy of capital punishment against the political crimes of the masses can still subsist? It is no longer a poor weak multitude, separated from the influential classes, whom it is now the question to reduce to impotence. Who would now treat the multitude, composed of students, merchants, master-workmen, and farmers, as it was treated formerly? It is there, however, that the evil would be if it burst forth; it is there that the remedy must be applied; and in order to give that remedy the direct utility which the government of Louis XIV. obtained, by hanging or chasing from the town of Rennes all the inhabitants of a turbulent street—in order to suppress the danger in the persons of its authors—what intensity, what extent would it not require to possess!

But what would be the consequences? Shall we say what disgust, what horror of government, would run through this electrical society, where everything is known, everything propagated, and where millions of men in the same condition, of the same sentiments, without having ever seen or spoken to each other, yet know reciprocally their fate, and in spite of the calm around them, feel themselves menaced by a storm growling at the distance of a hundred leagues from their canton. In such circumstances two conditions are attached to the physical efficacy of capital punishment—the first is, that it weighs heavily upon the place where the danger appears; and the other, that it does not carry desolation and confusion into the whole country. Formerly, these two conditions were united; but now this is impossible, and the authority which would fulfil the first would soon feel itself more compromised by the horror and agitation spread throughout the country, than reassured by the solitude it might have made in one corner of the state.

We cannot struggle against social facts: they have roots which the hand of man cannot reach, and when they have once taken possession of the soil, it is necessary to learn to live under their shadow. There are no longer great nobles to destroy, or a rabble to decimate. Physically useless against individuals, since there are none whose life is dangerous to government, capital punishment is equally so against the masses, who are too strong and too watchful to allow it to be exercised with efficacy. In this first point of view, then, capital punishment, as a direct means of suppressing danger, is vain: it is but a custom, a prejudice, a routine, derived from a time when, indeed, it did attain the end intended by really delivering power from its enemies. And power, which still retains this worn-out weapon, is itself aware of its vanity; for when it has to do with men of any consideration, it wisely hesitates to employ it; and when, on the other hand, it is a portion of the population which it fears, the impossibility is so evident, that it never dreams of employing so terrible an instrument.

The efficacy, then, of the punishment of death must be moral, since it is not physical. This is the strong point in which its friends confide: let us examine it.

3

MORAL EFFICACY OF CAPITAL PUNISHMENT.

Considered generally, and in its moral efficacy, capital punishment, like all other punishments, has a double effect—inspiring aversion to crime, and fear of chastisement. The two ideas—crime and chastisement—are associated in the mind of man. When crime is seen, punishment is expected; when punishment is seen, crime is presumed. Founded upon this natural fact, legislation proposes in punishing not only to terrify, but also to maintain and fortify in all minds the conviction of the perversity of the acts it punishes; and it is thus it would dissuade the people from crime, and make that punishment an example.

I even think that punishments are still more exemplary by the moral impression they make, than by the terror they inspire. The laws have more force in the consciences of men than in their fears. The public reprobation and shame attached to certain acts have more power in deterring, than the chastisement which may follow. Those who are acquainted with human nature will agree with me in this; and let those who doubt only suppose the moral stigma removed from actions reckoned criminal by our code, and then inquire whether all the skill of the police, and all the rigour of power, could suffice for their prevention. Fear, no doubt, has its part in the moral efficacy of punishments; but we should not exaggerate the power of this agent, or forget the more energetic one which works to the same result.

It has been said that the moral antipathy inspired by crime is not increased by the severity of the punishment. It is true that if the punishment appears excessive, if it revolts more than conciliates the moral sentiments, if it changes the horror of the crime into pity for the criminal, it loses its desired effect. It is not true, however, that fear alone arises from severe punishments, and that they do not move the conscience still more strongly: all this varies according to the times, ideas, and manners: the punishment which formerly spoke loudly against the crime might now speak only in favour of the criminal. Moreover, even in the midst of the mildest manners, pity never so exclusively possesses the heart of man that, while beholding a great punishment merited by a great crime, he suddenly forgets the crime, to think only of the sufferings of the criminal. Pity has its sentiment of justice; and when this justice is not offended, the gravity of the punishment exercises its power alike over the conscience and the fear. I do not dispute that capital punishment has this double virtue.

Neither do I believe that it now acts only by fear, or that it is, besides, so contrary to our manners that it fails as entirely in its end as would do the punishment of the wheel. I think even that, become rarer, its effect upon the imagination may have increased with the importance which a man's life takes in the public mind. But even as simple capital punishment preserves its moral efficacy, and as slow and cruel punishments have lost theirs, in like manner are introduced or developed such differences in crimes, that the same punishment does not possess the same efficacy in all.

Why does capital punishment, when applied to private crimes, such as murder, robbery, incendiarism, &c. never fail to produce this chief effect, the end of all punishments, which consists in increasing the aversion these crimes inspire? It is because it finds this aversion in all hearts, or at least because there is no dispute as to the natural criminality of the acts which it punishes. Two facts are certain—that the action made criminal by law has really taken place, and that it is really criminal. The public, power, even the accused, agree upon this. There is no question but to discover the author of an act of which no one contests the reality or the wickedness. Thus the first condition of the moral efficacy of punishment is in some sort fulfilled beforehand; it is a proved fact, which calls for chastisement, and the chastisement addresses itself to men who think in unison with the law.

In political crimes, on the contrary, these two circumstances are uncertain: it is not certain that the acts of the accused are really these which the law incriminates, nor that the acts incriminated by the law arc naturally and invariably criminal. The first uncertainty is evident: no one in the present day is ignorant that in the case of private offences it is the criminal alone who is sought out, the offence being certain; while in a political matter, such as conspiracies, offences of the press, &c. it is almost always necessary to discover in a series of actions more or less significant both the offence and the offender. As to the second uncertainty, let it not be said that in affirming that, it also exists, I wish to enervate the laws, and leave public order without a safeguard. I affirm only that the immorality of political crimes is neither so clear nor so immutable as that of private crimes; it is constantly metamorphosed or obscured by the vicissitudes of human affairs; it varies according to times, events, and the rights and merits of power; it totters every moment under the blows of a force which pretends to fashion it according to its caprices or its necessities. It would be difficult to find in the political world a meritorious and innocent act which has not received, in some corner of the world or of time, a legal incrimination. Who shall say that all these laws were in the right? Who affirm that they have always carried into the minds of the people the conviction of their justice, and inspired, together with fear of the punishment, horror of the crime?

Who will now become the absolute defender of passive obedience, and construe the rights of society as subordinate to the written law, whatever be the character of power? Such an attempt would be vain. In things so changeable and complicated, true morality does not allow itself to be thus absolutely fixed and imprisoned for ever in the text of the laws; and Providence, which so often delivers up to force the destiny of men, does not permit it thus to make and unmake crime and virtue at its pleasure. 'Do you not know,' said the president of the revolutionary tribunal to M. Engrand d'Alleray, 'the law which forbids the sending of money to emigrants?' 'Yes,' replied the old man, 'but I know of an older law which commands me to support my children.' This, which was true in 1793, will be so always, in spite of all codes, and in the face of all kinds of power. Doubtless there are real and odious political crimes; but those that are made by the laws are not always so, whatever the laws or times may be. Force exercises an immense empire over the weak mind of man; but it is not given to it to deprave it to this degree, that crimes of its own fashioning excite the instinctive antipathy attached to crimes declared as such by the true law. Tyranny apart, and even in tolerably regular times, there frequently rests upon actions of this kind a great moral uncertainty. When they raise in the public a violent animosity, it is perhaps because the public is passionate, and itself inclined to injustice; and when it is always incredulous, and secretly given to excuse them, it is because power displeases the public. Which is right, and which wrong? Force may prevent people from knowing, or at least from speaking, but in almost every case capital punishment in political crimes fails to produce, either surely or generally, the really moral impression which accompanies it in private crimes.

An analogous difference exists between these two classes of crimes as to the effect of the fear sought to be inspired by capital punishment. The robber and the murderer are isolated in society, or at least their friends, protectors, or accomplices are only robbers or murderers like themselves. This they know; and when punishment overtakes them, it is not power alone, but the whole of society, which arms itself against them. With society they were at war, and it has conquered. This victory gives the idea of an immense force directed against individuals, who can only oppose to it their courage or address. They will never have better fortune; never will a portion of the public embrace their cause; never will a day of triumph or vengeance dawn for them. They live in the midst of society like wild beasts in a country crowded by man, finding everywhere snares or enemies; without support, without shelter, and without other force than their personal strength, which every one attacks, and living in a fear which every one increases; and every condemnation, every execution of their brethren which takes place, is to them a solemn proof of the weakness of their position, and a warning of the fate which awaits them.

But the enemies of a government, men inclined to conspire, or who do actually conspire, are in a very different position: they do not cease to belong to society, and they are attached to some party, to whose assistance and protection they look. This party may not wish what they wish, and may not believe what they believe; but what of that? They merely exaggerate its power, and misapprehend its intentions. In the meantime they live surrounded by men whose desires assimilate with their own, and whose illusions respond to their confidence. Who does not know what prodigious blindness possesses political factions, and with what mad certainty each reckons upon its strength and success? In each passer-by, under each roof from which the smoke rises, the robber sees an enemy; while the conspirator dreams everywhere of allies, and is confident of obtaining everywhere at least a temporary protection. And besides, if the latter is in danger, defenders will not fail him; his offence will be considered doubtful, and power unjust and violent; a thousand kind sentiments, a thousand wise reasons, will lend their support to designs which are disapproved of, and to conduct which is blamed, but which men cannot, and will not, allow to be suppressed by iniquity. Finally, if the man falls, it will not be in this isolation, in the midst of this universal animadversion, which freezes the most audacious courage. Perhaps in a future day he will be avenged; and in this expectation his friends regard his ruin as a blow from which the strength they possess, with the aid of a little more good fortune or prudence, may henceforth preserve them.

It is not possible to intimidate a faction like a band of robbers: in order to give in such cases the moral efficacy to capital punishment which it derives from fear, and which in a matter of private crime a single execution suffices to obtain, it would be necessary to go almost so far as to render its efficacy likewise physical; and we have seen that this has obstacles still more formidable, and dangers still more serious. There is, then, no analogy of this kind between private and political crimes, which are separated by profound differences. The question is not to examine the moral efficacy of capital punishment in general; because, whether it addresses itself to the conscience or fear, it will not produce the same effect in conspiracies as in robberies. It is necessary to confine ourselves exclusively to the former class of offences, in order to appreciate its influence. There, as in other cases, it proposes for itself the double end which every punishment aims at: it would prevent the evil, in making the crime detestable and the chastisement terrible.

I have just said that political crimes are of such a description that their moral perversity is more doubtful, more variable, and less generally recognised than that of private crimes; the punishment, therefore, whatever it may be, has a work here to perform which is spared it elsewhere. When some act of the kind is proclaimed to be criminal, men are not found, as in the case of murder or robbery, decided upon its character. Convictions must be changed, and a struggle entered into not only against passions, but against ideas; and as the question is to act upon those very men who would be inclined to commit what is thus proscribed, the difficulty becomes immense. In the present state of manners, the destitute, the vagabond, or the depraved, whatever be the unhappiness of their situation, or the vice of their inclinations, never believe that they are morally permitted to rob. Everything inculcates the interdict, and recalls it to them when they forget it; and the law finds very rarely, even in them, a belief directly opposed to right. Men carried to political offences, on the contrary, are enemies alike to the convictions and commands of the law; for the law affirms the established order to be good, while they think it bad; its continuance necessary, while they desire its fall; its existence sacred, while they demand its overthrow. No point of contact exists between these men and the law which addresses them; no common principle unites them; and to obtain obedience otherwise than through fear, the law must begin by making them believe it. Before obtaining this chief and powerful efficacy, which consists in fortifying the natural antipathy to crime, punishments are here encountered by an unaccustomed obstacle. They have not, in general, to do with beliefs; they are themselves a sanction to public belief, acting upon men who have transgressed while believing. How can the sanction of a principle produce its effect in a case where the principle does not exist! It may prove the strength of an enemy, but not the justice of its cause. Great questions recur everywhere. If Providence had imposed on human actions no other curb than fear of consequences—if men entirely abandoned to the counsel of their interest or the voice of their desires, were without those convictions which introduce order into the tumult of passion, and light into the uncertainties of life—chaos would soon invade the world, and the only means of maintaining order would be the sudden abasement of our nature by the absolute loss of its liberty. But man, by his moral convictions, binds and adapts himself to the will of Providence: he is in direct communication with it, comprehends the language of its laws, admits its principles, and submits himself to them freely; and notwithstanding the struggles which agitate him, notwithstanding his constant errors, there is no need of force to substitute slavery for obedience.

What man would be in his relations with Providence if his moral principles were to fail him, men inclined to political offences pretty nearly are in their relations with power. They do not believe what it believes; they have no wish for what it wishes; they contest with it even the legitimacy of its existence. How must power act upon them? It has sense enough to understand that force alone will not suffice, that it has never had enough of this to exterminate or imprison any considerable portion of the society it governs. It must change its dispositions, and re-establish between it and them this community, if not of intentions, at least of beliefs, which gives law its true empire, arming it with the power to prevent a hundred crimes by punishing a single one, and raising its administrators to the rank of teachers of the people, whereas formerly they tried in vain to remain their jailers.

Of all the means which power employs for attaining this end, punishments assuredly are the least efficacious. Punishment supposes crime, and if the supposition is not admitted, the moral efficacy of the former disappears. When the man on whom the punishment is inflicted, and those who think with him, judge that he is unjustly smitten, in this case punishment has the effect of injustice: it irritates, confirms the hostile opinion, widens the breach between the law and its transgressors, and thus goes directly against a part of its own purpose. But if, on the contrary, the enemies of power admit that it is right in punishing them, if they see that it employs its force against them with reason, they can only have taken the part of considering themselves in a state of war. From that moment every social tie is broken; the question is no longer of laws or chastisements; plots are ambuscades, and punishments defeats. Government has lost its moral position: it has descended to an equality of force; everything is equal between it and its enemies: as it has the right of self-defence, they have the right of attack: the claim of obedience on one side, and justice on the other, are equally false. All this belongs to society, but society is dissolved: there is nothing now but war, with the liberty of its arms, the continuity of its dangers, and the uncertainty of its results.

Of all punishments, capital punishment is that whose employment precipitates parties and power most rapidly into this last situation: it brings war to mind by rousing violent animosities, and provoking vengeance. It is therefore the punishment which possesses least of all the kind of efficacy we are now in quest of. This efficacy, I repeat, has for its condition the reform of certain ideas: it will not bear its fruit till the men it addresses consent to consider those acts culpable from which it would dissuade them; at least they must have conceived doubts on the subject, and the notion of the legitimacy of power must have entered their minds.

It has often been attempted to introduce moral convictions by means of punishments, but when these have not succeeded in exterminating, they have always failed. It is said that moral convictions are not aimed at—that the struggle is only against vicious desires, inordinate wants, and criminal interests. But this is a mistake: for when the morality or immorality of an action is not evident, when there is room for the least uncertainty, then passions, interests, everything, hide themselves under opinions, and all resolve or metamorphose themselves into ideas. The most perverse and headstrong of men are disinclined to dispense with reason, and content themselves with brute force. They have ever a wish to legitimise in their own eyes even the least disinterested conduct; they carefully collect every motive, every pretext, and seize upon the slightest pretence; and what is more easy, after an unexpected overthrow, to form thus for themselves a creed which lends its support to hostility against power? Was there ever a true faction that was anything else than a union of banditti forced on by their own base interests, and accessible only to fear? The weakest government of our day might hold such a danger cheap; but punishments are desired to act in a very different sphere: to teach the citizens that it is culpable to conspire against established order, and deliver their country to the terrible chances of revolution. Be it known, however, that punishments have no power to propagate such ideas; they must already exist in the mind. It is weakness to suppose that they can be reaped when other causes have not yet sown them: this is attributing to punishments a power which they do not possess: they cannot make things be detested as criminal which are regarded as meritorious, nor can they demonstrate the moral legitimacy of power: they have no effect upon the established convictions of the people; and when these are hostile to authority, it is by other means than punishments that government can succeed in changing them, and when they will not change, punishments, instead of reforming, only strengthen their empire. Let us talk no more, then, of capital punishment preventing political crimes by inspiring a hatred of them: this really moral efficacy, however powerful against ordinary crimes, is here without reality; and the more vigorous parties become, and the more the perils of power increase, the less pretence can capital punishment make to such salutary influence. It is, then, both for government and the factious, only another step in antagonism, and for the public only another blow of destiny, fatal to the vanquished to-day, and perhaps to the conqueror to-morrow. Does it act more powerfully through fear? I have already shown that in this point of view, and by the sole difference of social position existing between conspirators and robbers, political crimes offer to the laws much less hold than private offences. But this is not the only cause which renders the terror of punishment less efficacious in political matters than is commonly supposed.

Men are influenced by different motives; and there must be an agreement between them and the means used for control. Who does not know that he cannot speak to a man whom interest governs in the same manner as he would speak to him who is ruled by passion, or to a man who is possessed by passion as to him who is directed by an opinion or a duty? We study carefully, in the private relations of life, those various dispositions of mankind, and never think of addressing ourselves to feelings which have no existence. The legislator who acts upon the masses cannot arrive at this nice justice, this special fitness of things; but he need not commit the profound absurdity of directing the same means indifferently against dispositions the most different; and since he can avoid this, it is imperative upon him to do so, not only for the sake of justice, but for the sake of success.

Fear, for example, has more efficacy against interests than passions, and against passions than ideas: it is easier to prevent a poor man from stealing than an irritated man from seeking vengeance; and the angry man, in his turn, is more easily restrained than the fanatic who believes himself commanded to assassinate. Generally, when a man's governing principle is of a nature in some sort material, such as a purely personal interest, fear has much power: it opposes interest to interest, and all happens thus in the same sphere; for there is similitude and fitness in the impelling and opposing motive. As we approach the moral order, fear loses its virtue: it ceases to be in natural and direct relation with the impulses it would repress; it addresses them in a language not their own, gives them reasons they cannot admit, and thus falls short of the mark it aims at. But when we arrive at the purest and rarest of all motives, at the full and dominating convictions of our moral nature, fear remains without action upon the man thus placed above that world to which its power is confined.

And this is not a theory: it is a series of facts, regulated by Providence, which has willed that material and moral order shall remain distinct and profoundly different even in their union.

To which category do these causes of action belong which generally urge men to political offences? Here, also, the diversity is great; for I am far from believing that everything happens within the moral order, or even upon its confines. Among the causes which excite hostility to power are ideas, passions, and interests: here honourable sentiments or sincere beliefs, there frenzied desires or the most brutal selfishness. All these principles of action join, are confounded together, and form in their admixture a heterogeneous force, whose different elements cannot be combated by the same arms, nor be repressed by the same means.

I do not say that the fear inspired by the spectacle, or the chance of capital punishment, is without efficacy to prevent the explosions of this confused force: but I do say that its efficacy is not of a simple nature; and that even if it finds in the adversary it combats points where it can strike with success, there will be others which it cannot reach, and where its rebound will produce a contrary effect to that contemplated by the penal law.

When Charles II., urged on by the Catholics, and by his own taste for absolute power, resorted to condemnations and punishments, the opposition included, as always happens, the most heterogeneous elements. The followers of the republic joined those of Cromwell; and the fanaticism of the Puritans did not refuse an alliance with men whose disgust of frequently-ridiculous controversies had rendered them indifferent to every religious belief. To men revolted by the license of the court were joined others influenced by the love of disorder, the melancholy fruit of revolutions; and the ambitious who sought after popularity, for the sake of wealth or power, stood side by side with sincere patriots, disinterested friends of their country's liberty: thus Lord Shaftesbury voted with Lord Russell. In the same party, in fine, met together the most noble sentiments and the most culpable passions, the most sincere beliefs and the most worldly interests, the highest virtue and the most shameful desires.

What must have been, what really was, the effect of political rigour upon a party thus composed? The court triumphed at first: for those who had joined the party from interest withdrew from it; the venal sold themselves; the timid sunk into silence; old republicans, in thus losing their illusions, believed liberty lost without retrieve; Monk corrupted or abandoned his former companions; and Shaftesbury fled to Holland. Fear reigned in all its glory. But at the same time that it struck the vulnerable portion of the party, it deeply and irreconcilably offended forces which it was not its business to attack. If cowards were afraid, brave men became indignant; and if fear brought over to the court some deserters from the popular party, it likewise confirmed the people in their aversion; causing the former to think themselves in error in having attacked power, and proving to the latter their right to do so. The reformers were alienated past return; the passions, kept in check perhaps among the great, grew furious in the rabble; the public mistrust became incurable; and all the friends of national liberty judged themselves in peril. As to the more ambitious of the party, Lord Russell and Sidney were the most unfortunate of the conspirators: they became martyrs for the people; and time soon showed that if fear had borne fruits favourable for power, it had likewise sowed some that were very bitter.

Such is, in a political matter, the inevitable condition of the indirect efficacy of punishment. It is not confined to the limits in which it can be of service; it does not restrict its operation to perils which it can combat with success; but in some cases causes the desired effect, and in others one which would rather have been avoided: its influence can neither be diverted nor even foreseen. It is a weapon of unknown power, which, thrown at random, may strike one required point, and at the same time in a hundred others excite new enemies and new dangers.

The want of reflection in men explains everything: but that power which, in order to destroy political factions, calls to its aid the fear of death, commits a strange mistake; for in employing this means, it knows not what it does. It should at least, before having recourse to it, consider what is the nature of the danger it fears, what the interior composition of the factions it combats, and what will be the effects, so variable and complicated, of the punishment of death. If the question was now of such enemies as in the thirteenth century were those of established governments; if political struggles carried physical disorder suddenly into society, and the gatherings of conspirators threatened always to turn into bands of robbers, then fear would be the true weapon. If even, in our day, we dealt with seditions engendered among the multitude, provoked by some brutal passion or some physical interest—by the most pressing, for instance, the most excusable of interests, famine—there, again, I could conceive the employment of the punishment of death. It might, indeed, be needlessly and odiously abused; but it would at least be used with a knowledge of its effects against an evil to which its fear might be properly applied. Parties now, however, are very differently constituted: they unite men of all conditions, rich and poor, idle and industrious, peaceable and disorderly, bound together by numerous and systematic relations. If conspiracies do not obtain entire success, and change the face of empires, they seldom advance so far as they attempt. We live in a society recently overturned, where legitimate and illegitimate interests, honourable and blameable sentiments, just and false ideas, are so mingled, that it is very difficult to strike hard without striking wrong. We are an ancient people entering into a new social order; the errors of inexperience are seen amidst the security of civilisation; all is obscure and confused, without being entirely disorderly or violent. In such a state of men and things, to believe in the efficacy of capital punishment against political danger, and to rely on the fear it inspires as a great means of government, is to mistake both the evil and the remedy, and to employ arms at once old and poisonous, which are no longer of use, and cannot be handled without danger.

I find everywhere the same mistake; and it is by confounding times that means are misunderstood. In the former constitution of society, the moral efficacy of capital punishment was powerfully seconded by its direct and physical efficacy. When it fell upon the chief of an eminent party, known to all its members, and invested with immense power, his personal fall not only dissipated a great danger, but struck terror into the whole faction, and it was said on all hands—How has this man fallen? What! were not all his riches, his credit, his numerous followers, and his strong places, able to defend him? His adversaries are then much to be dreaded! How is it possible to escape their power? How strive against that which has destroyed such a man? Beyond the circle of political conflicts the same phenomenon is visible. The death of Cartouche or Mandrin will be a much greater example, and act much more powerfully upon robbers, than that of an obscure pickpocket. If you descend into the rabble, you will find the same relation between the moral and physical efficacy of punishments; for there the number of the victims makes up for their want of celebrity. Is it surprising that the population of a district should be paralysed with fear when they see their ranks thinned by chastisements, and encounter at every step the instruments or the ruins of this devastating power? Sepulture itself is refused to their remains, and the dead remain above ground to terrify the living.

At such a price is obtained that fear which in former times derived its terrible influence from capital punishment. If you try now to restore the vanished régime, you will not be able to fulfil the conditions; you will not be able to multiply political punishments so as to terrify by their number. A government aiming at such effects would find danger moving against it at the same pace as fear among the people. Society no longer furnishes those victims whose illustrious fall spread terror everywhere. You must act here and there against some obscure wretches, whose names are unheard, and who are known only by their misfortune. And how can you destroy such men? Not by the force of power: the conflict is too unequal. By its justice? Have a care: when interest is personal, and the superiority so immense, justice is very open to suspicion: if doubt is possible, you may count upon its becoming in many minds equivalent to a certainty. And what fear have you then inspired? Not the fear of force, but of iniquity; and a government, in my opinion, can gain nothing from the one without the other.

That, however, is the error which possesses those who, in our day, rely upon the punishment of death: they mistake the nature of the fear they spread, and believe themselves to have proved their strength when they have but made their justice or their wisdom doubtful. Strength is not so easily proved, nor always in the same manner.

Two governments have ruled France despotically—the Convention, which reigned by political punishments; and Bonaparte, who made little use of them, and even took pains to avoid them. Both, by different means, were powerful, and dreaded. But was the scaffold the only strength of the Convention? No rational man can believe it: it played its part, just like conflagrations, or falling houses, or ravaging banditti; but in all these the efforts are greater than the energy, and the Convention, consuming itself almost as quickly as its enemies, fell into the abyss from which it issued; for in vain is power great—the crime by which it triumphs destroys it in our day more rapidly than ever. Bonaparte was strong in his turn; but it was not by punishments that he proved his strength, and made it to be feared. He punished some conspiracies, suppressed others, and passed over many more; he even specially passed over those which proceeded from the party opposed to the Revolution. Invested with power by the need of order and justice, and in opposition to the anarchical tyranny of the Jacobins, already worn out, he comprehended well that he must invoke power from the same interests and sentiments which had just procured him the Empire. The need of order within and of victory without the Empire had made the 18th Brumaire, and Bonaparte reigned as he had risen—by order and victory; and when by his faults he had lost or compromised victory in Europe, and security in France, he fell, still full of life, but having ceased to be strong.

If I may use the figure, there is a star which bestows their strength upon governments, and which they are not at liberty to choose or renounce without danger. They are born and live with a nature of their own, but in a situation they have not made, and under conditions they cannot direct; and their skill consists in becoming acquainted with these, and adapting themselves to them. Thus are they powerful—one by war, another by peace; this by severity, and that by gentleness—according as the different means of government have affinity with the especial laws of their destiny. And if they misunderstand these laws, and mistake the means of the government which correspond with them; if they imagine they can attempt indifferently any path they choose, and set in motion such or such a spring according to their fancy; if they consider power as an arsenal of all sorts of arms, equally useful to all comers—then their star abandons them: they hesitate, waver, try in vain a thousand resources, which fail them successively, and feeling themselves growing weaker day by day, are foolishly astonished that a course of conduct which has succeeded so well with others does nothing but increase their embarrassments and perils.

What was the star of the Restoration? Under what native laws was the present government placed? Where were its elements of power, and what means of action were fitted to its position and its nature? I would know this, in order to discover if capital punishment in political matters is really an arm for its use, and which preserves in its hands, both as regards its own interest and that of the people, a salutary efficacy. I cannot help the question becoming so extensive. I shall endeavour to keep within its bounds; but it is very necessary that I follow wherever it conducts me.

4

THE SAME SUBJECT CONTINUED.

I shall say but one word of external matters. The Restoration found war in France, and France, like Europe, weary of war. This was both for France and Europe a pledge of peace. Peace was then the general law of our destiny; and in it should France have sought its power, and likewise its dignity, for the one is not separated from the other, at least for long.

Within, the Restoration found neither anarchy, impiety, contempt for the laws, struggles between classes, nor any of those revolutionary scourges of which they now speak, as if they had possessed France for twenty-five years without interruption. This is not true. The old nobility lived at peace with the new, and both with the nation. Vanity had its folly as well as its pleasures, and the country thought little about the matter. Unluckily for our prospects and our rights—I thought so then, and do so still—power was at least strongly constituted, and in such a manner that disorder was not to be feared either for us or itself. Moral disorder, that internal shamelessness which incredulity produces, that domestic license, contempt for all existing forms of things, and aversion to every rule and restraint, had disappeared. Order, an imperious and blind necessity in 1799, was in 1814 a habit and a general taste, and the Restoration found it so.

It is true that order, not only politically, but morally, was without guarantees. In political respects, no real and independent institutions subsisted by their own strength, capable of protecting either the general interests against individual pretensions, or individual interests against the tyranny of general interests and the natural vices or errors of power. One man had sufficed for many, and had pretended to suffice for all. In falling, he left power entirely naked and defenceless: for it had rights, and no means of exercising them; strength, and no means of displaying it; wants, and no means of providing for them by its own efforts.

In moral respects the evil was less apparent, but still real and profound. Order reigned in social facts, and even in manners; but the principles of order were not in the soul. These principles I may sum up in two words: the firm sentiment of right and true belief. These were almost alike wanting. I will not say that in the respect for religion and morals which replaced the revolutionary cynicism there was hypocrisy, but still there was not sincerity: it was an external respect, founded upon necessities and conveniences, not upon convictions and sentiments. People considered it good, and observed it, but without having in themselves that which occasions it, and without troubling themselves as to its legitimate nature. The head of the government set the example; but if he desired its habits, he feared its principles; for while ridiculing ideas, he acknowledged their empire. Discipline without moral rule, obedience with indifference, this is all he sought, and society gradually took the character under his hand. Never had order been at once so exact, and yet so foreign, to the inner life of man; and never had there been so much regularity united with so little faith.

As for the idea of right, it was raised little above civil relations; beyond which force reigned so supreme, that it seemed as if right belonged to it alone. When there exists in a nation a will before which everything disappears, or is reduced to silence, the sentiment of right perishes; and if this will is at the same time very active, and is possessed with the passion for displaying itself on every side, in war, in peace, manifesting itself everywhere, and considering every obstacle as illegitimate, it exercises over men the most formidable corruption they can be subject to, for it deprives them of the power and even thought of resisting—that is to say, takes from them their moral existence. Right is the right of resistance: there is no other; for take that away, and every other disappears. Bonaparte struck them all to the heart, at least in their relations with his power; and thus repulsing beliefs on the one hand, and rights on the other, he carried away from the order which he maintained, without having founded it, every guarantee but habit and his own will.

What Bonaparte did not give, the Restoration could give us: this was at once its mission and its nature. It was its mission, for a government has no other than that of satisfying the wants of the society in which it is established; not only the permanent and universal wants of society, but likewise, and above all perhaps, the special wants of its epoch. But even as Bonaparte had had to bring back external order, and to cause the cessation, by the despotism of a single will, of the anarchy of individual wills, so the Restoration, taking things where Bonaparte left them, had to infuse into external order the belief which constitutes moral order, and to replace the empire of will by the empire of right. Though less visible, these wants are not the less real; they are found at the bottom of every legitimate aspiration of every party.

It was also in the nature of the Restoration to respond to them. And from the first it was constrained to the institutions of liberty. I make use of this word, for it appears to me the only one by which the imperious necessity for the Charter can be expressed. Such constraints are not offensive to the power to which they apply, for it is Providence which directs them. The mistrust which the Restoration could not fail to excite exacted guarantees which liberty alone could offer. Thus liberty was perhaps still more necessary to the Restoration than power to the Consulate: but it is in the bosom of liberty that public beliefs are developed; it is under its shadow that general ideas germinate and grow, ideas adapted to the time and to the instinct of minds, and called forth and gathered by the secret wants of an entire people. Despotism never produces them; and the great convictions which have governed the world are never formed but against power or in a free state. The idea and the sentiment of right spring of necessity from liberty. This does not need proof, especially in modern times, when the bloody combats of the little

Greek or Italian factions would not be, in the eyes of any one, liberty.

And this is not all: that which was a necessity to the Restoration was likewise analogous to its nature: it drew its force not from force itself, but from an idea. The word legitimacy has been, and will still be, much abused. One loses much by this abuse; for in trying to make it mean what it does not, we run the risk of depriving it of what it really contains of truth and strength. It expresses a right, real and obvious, though limited as rights always are, when existing simultaneously with other rights. This right has made the strength of the Restoration, and even the Restoration itself. The Restoration was the result of the influence which recollections of long possession and certain moral principles and sentiments accompanying them exercise upon the minds of men. Whatever we may think of right— its origin, conditions, limits—we should know that it is a fact, a powerful fact, and one which was felt as such by Cromwell and William III., as well as in the reign of Charles II.

It is the consequence of this fact that, founded as it is upon a moral idea, and sustained by those which are joined to or derived from it, the development of its force must be sought especially in the moral order where its principle resides. Elicited by convictions effected in virtue of a right, convictions and rights were at the Restoration the natural means of government. Subject to necessity even in the moment of triumph, obliged to yield in returning to the Revolution, it dreaded what the Revolution desired—it had to conciliate antagonistic principles and rights; but even that was a moral work foreign to its direct action, and which new sentiments and new ideas could alone accomplish.

Bonaparte had rebuilt the altars, and restored its solemnities to public worship; and notwithstanding revolutionary clamours, the non-Catholics felt no alarm. After the Restoration, Catholicism came to demand, and liberty of conscience to fear much more. What had the Restoration to do to defend society and itself from this peril? Could it, like the Revolution, or even like Bonaparte, treat different communions now with severity, now with complacency, and arbitrarily restrain or permit their action? No: that would have been opposed to the general nature of its institutions, and have shocked the respect it owed to faith as well as to liberty. Another path was open to it: and that was, to lay vigorous hold upon the principles of religious liberty, to proclaim it in all its acts, to inculcate it in every mind, and to make it, in fine, one of its doctrines of government, one of its public creeds which, really adopted, are found everywhere acting by their own virtue, and maintaining order almost of themselves. All the wants of the new order prescribed to the Restoration such a course; and it had, partly in the necessities of its situation, and partly in its nature, what sufficed for this noble task. The protection accorded to religious and moral ideas was not, on its part, the confession of an error, for all these ideas rallied spontaneously around it. The respect in which rights were held was of great importance to it, for it drew its own title from a right; and the maintenance of the public liberties was not less its policy than their establishment, for it could not, like Bonaparte, pretend to despotism by victory. It was, in fine, its condition and its destiny to rule especially by the moral influences, to aid in their development, to base on their empire the order which it found restored, and to have recourse to force but rarely, and then with regret, as a means foreign to its nature, and the necessity of which rendered its employment grievous.

If we consider the occasions when the present government has tried this means, we shall be convinced, without difficulty, that the natural laws which rule it have had little to do with its use. Sometimes, as in the slightest popular agitations, we have seen it used with a precipitation and to an extent which exhibited less skill than inquietude; sometimes, as in the proceedings of the Cour des Pairs, indications of severity were observable sufficient to inspire much alarm, but which ended merely in correctional punishments. The movement has almost always appeared above the cause, and the effect beneath the movement. I do not know if a neutral observer is in the right to judge thus; but assuredly the employment of force, and the public threats of severity, have failed both in motive and address; and many believe that power has made use of them either wrongfully or unskilfully. Either of these faults would prove that the means of governing are improper.

It is not merit to succeed by force even at the moment when it is invoked; but what government does not come to the end of its means? It is still necessary that, after having set it at work, it leaves it public, convinced that this was necessary; and that it has used the means so well as to render this need more rare. If the first of its convictions fail, power is suspected of timidity and malevolence; if the second, it is taxed with want of skill, and its employment of force has weakened instead of strengthening it.

I will not go farther; I have said enough to show in what system of government the Restoration seemed to me born, and how, in trying to leave it, it would lose its advantages without acquiring those of a different system. It cannot strengthen itself more by judicial rigour than by conquests. If fear ever became the machinery of its power—if, in order to maintain itself, it was necessary to terrify the interests, opinions, and sentiments it suspected—the more pressing would be the need, the more useless would be the weapon, and the danger would increase with the necessity. Our government, then, can still less than other governments rely upon the indirect efficacy of capital punishment. Rarely simple, and often in the complication of its effects more hurtful than profitable, this means would carry into the present régime more trouble than security. No one in France or in Europe will ever think that the Restoration is called upon to crush all it may fear. It has not been able to give such proofs of its physical force, that the minds of men submit as a matter of course to its frequent use. When it strikes, many people are tempted to believe it more severe than just, or more in danger than it is in reality, and its strokes awaken less the idea of its energy than of its danger. More than one government, after great severities, has been considered still weak; and in such case it finds itself in the worst of conditions—that of a power whose weakness provokes conspiracy, and which tries afterwards to fill up, by means of punishments, the abysses which that weakness has opened. The reason is, that force must exist before it pretends to inspire fear; and in the case of the Restoration, the sources of force must be sought for elsewhere than in the means of terror. I repeat that power itself has now an instinct of this; for it has not, while administering death-punishment, that confidence, that certainty of success, which is almost its only guarantee. It causes, yet fears the sentiments this melancholy spectacle may excite, without feeling assured of the terror it wishes to inspire; and this instinct is not a mistake, but the voice of nature. It is bound to moderation in punishment, just as in its exterior relations it is bound to peace. The Charter has abolished confiscation, and the Restoration justly honours the Charter. I do not demand the abolition of capital punishment; but I am convinced that, against its enemies, government gains nothing by this agent, and would gain much by showing itself very niggardly in its use.

It can no longer have a physical and direct efficacy. Its moral efficacy is not so great in political as in private offences; it is powerless in inspiring aversion to crime; it is equivocal and mixed with the most various results when tending to the propagation of fear; and it is more feeble, more uncertain, and more perilous to the present government than to powers of a different origin and position. Is this enough? It would be well were this all. But many other reasons, and many more dangers, suggest themselves; and these I shall proceed to indicate.

5

DOUBLE CHARACTER OF THE GOVERNMENT.

What power seeks in the employment of capital punishment is security. I have shown that this it does not find; but that it often finds what it does not seek, and what it should and always does wish to avoid.

There are some simple truths which no one disputes, which good sense immediately admits, and yet which are no sooner admitted than forgotten. The reason is, perhaps, that being adopted without debate, we are not led to think of their consequences.

Here is a truth of this kind. Every government has a double character. Charged with maintaining public order and justice, and conducting the affairs of the state, it represents the social interest. Formed of men, and thus liable to the passions and vices of our nature, it has, besides, a personal interest, which is, to execute its will, and preserve at any price its existence.

That these two characters are united in power, that the one is legitimate, and the other illegitimate, and that institutions have for their object the constraining of the government to act by the former, and to fortify the people from the perils of the latter, who will deny? Who would even insinuate a doubt? Power itself would not dare to do so. But in this instance power forgets what it would not for a moment deny.

From the fact, that it is only called upon to act in the social interest, while it still preserves a distinct personal interest, proceeds this consequence, that all it does in virtue of the former character fortifies it, and all it does in that of the latter weakens it.

However frequently misunderstood, this is evident. I do not speak of legitimacy, nor of justice, nor of any moral obligation. Independently of every motive of this kind, it is clear that if power acts only for its own sake, in the sole interest of its will or durability, it separates itself from society, courts a risk of detection, and if detected, exposes itself to being forsaken or even attacked by that general force from which its own has sprung.

That prudence prescribes to power to show itself ever in its social, and dissemble its individual aspect, and that it is of importance to its existence to appear on every occasion the representative of the public interest, and not the minister of its own, would serve to show, if it were necessary to show, its continual efforts to appear what it is not, and to pass for the organ of society even when it acts against its wants or wishes.

To abjure its personal, in order to retain its social character, would be, on the part of power, an act of the highest virtue. To convince the people that it acts only in the general interest, and binds up its destiny in theirs, would be its greatest art. To keep itself apart, preoccupied with its own affairs, and in all the nakedness of its distinct existence, would be foolish and perilous in the extreme.

There was a time when governments could so act with less danger. When they drew their revenues from their own domains, when they possessed their places of war like an estate, when they formed armies of adventurers, attracted by the pay alone, and pledged to serve everywhere, then power had a separate existence, and a distinct form from that of society. If skilful, it still tried to identify itself with the country, and so received from it a much greater strength; but if incapable or passionate, it could isolate itself at least for a time, to live on its own funds, and preserve some reality whilst losing its public character, and allowing its personal sentiments and interests to predominate in its acts and language.

But this time is past: power, which cannot live of itself, can no longer live by itself. Everything draws it towards society. Does it want money!—society must give it: laws?—society must approve of them. If it acts, its acts arc judged; if it speaks, its words are commented on: the public weighs constantly upon it by the rule of necessity. As the representative of society, its strength may be great, greater than ever; but if special and isolated, it is a cipher. Alone to-day, it will be nothing tomorrow.

It has, then, the greatest interest in avoiding every appearance of egotism, and in making its public character obviously predominate over its individual one.

But there are traits which belong to one more than the other of these characters, symptoms which reveal the latter, but not the former. The employment of capital punishment politically is of this kind. It announces the predominance of the personal existence of power over its social existence, and shows it to be occupied with itself, and combating a peril which perhaps threatens only itself. And what is more natural? When we look at history, and ask why so much blood has been shed on the political scaffold, it is seldom that the spirit of past society rises to reply, 'That blood was shed for me.' Governments almost always present themselves alone to give account of these punishments: their own passions, faults, interests, commanded them; and next to the victims themselves, society suffered most. I know that the prospect of this future responsibility troubles power but little, and less because it is perverse, than because, like men, it is reckless; but we have at least gathered from it this knowledge, that the necessities of a power which kills, often false with regard to itself, are almost always so with regard to society; and that if it must kill in its own defence, that defence is necessary merely because it willed those things which suited no interest but its own.

This knowledge, little disseminated formerly, and almost confined to moralists, is now popular; it has become a sort of instinct, which reveals to us, in all their extent, the position and the illusions of power. When it is said that the illusions of what we call monarchy are dissipated, and its prestiges vanished, we know not how much to believe. It is not, however, in reality, a question of illusions and prestiges; it is that things themselves are changed: every sphere of existence or of action is enlarged; and that which was particular has become general, not only for society and its guarantees, but for the government and its profit. The citizen whose affairs took him little from his corporation, whose thoughts rarely wandered beyond the walls of his town, now knows himself to be engaged and compromised in affairs of the highest importance, and in the most complicated deliberations. The words *judgment of the state, political necessity*, which formerly struck upon his ear without his comprehending their sense, although he admitted their dominion, awaken ideas within him which trouble, and sentiments which agitate him. He has indeed reason to be moved more than formerly; for this government, which then had its sphere apart, higher and greater, but also more special and restricted, has itself become much more general, more directly, more universally associated with the interests and life of every citizen. Does it require money?—It demands it from all. Does it make laws?—They are for all. Has it fear?—All maybe its object. The distinctions in the nature of great and small exist no longer for power: its relations are with the magistrates of a village, as well as with the chiefs of the state; it has to produce an effect everywhere, and everywhere receives some motive of action.

And what is astonishing in the fact of the condition of government and the disposition of the people having changed? These changes are reciprocal, and correspond with each other. If power is no longer a mystery to society, the reason is, that society has ceased to be so to power: if authority meets everywhere with minds that pretend to judge it, it is because it comes into daily contact with these minds: if they demand that its conduct shall be on every occasion legitimate, it is because it has the disposal of all the strength of the country: if the public busies itself more with the government, government likewise acts over a very different public, and power is enhanced as well as liberty.

Of what, then, do you complain? Have you so little ambition that this displeases you! It is true you have lost the independence which belongs to a private life: your passions, and your personal interests, can no more have a place in the new order which surrounds you; you may not listen to their voice without its being known, nor obey their dictates without the reproach of failing in your mission. But what a mission is yours! If you are in harmony with society, the whole of society is concentrated and reflected in you. It is whilst offering itself entirely to you, that it asks you to live only for it. Formerly, you could confide only in a factitious policy, emanating from the ideas or desires of a single man, and tormenting nations to adapt them to designs they knew nothing about. But now policy must be true—that is to say, national—and that restrains the capricious actions or arbitrary conceptions of individuals. But what strength, what lustre, what energy belongs to a true national policy! What power is the best—that which represents the interests and the will of a people, or that which accomplishes only the thoughts, and responds only to the interest, of a man! I own I have no hesitation in deciding.

Hesitation, however, is of little consequence. I only insist at present upon this new state of society, to prove that power is not free to choose; and that if its conduct were to appear dictated by the necessities of its personal situation, rather than those of the social, which should be manifested in it, it would soon fall into a profound weakness; for society would soon be aware that it was separated from the fate as well as interest of the public, and acted only for itself. And how can it be supposed that capital punishment, employed politically, will not awaken this idea in society! There are fearful times, I know, when the people themselves call for and excuse it. I do not believe nations to be secure from those frightful maladies which engender human passions and errors. But a crisis of this kind is rare, and not of long duration; and it is precisely when it does take place that capital punishment becomes most odious. Remember the burst of kindly feeling with which France turned towards the emigrants in spite of all mistrust, past animosities, and every possible prejudice, the revolutionary policy was overturned, because it could neither become just nor remain cruel.

Since that period, capital punishment has been in political hands a weapon which compromises power more than serves it, and to which power has scarcely ever recourse but when in peril on its own account and from its own errors. It might be said that society, terrified by what it has seen, will no longer accept the responsibility of any political punishment, but is determined to believe that if it must be employed, government alone has need of an instrument which its own faults have rendered necessary. And that is especially true of a government which is not of yesterday, but has already held out, and is able to take its true position. If it were now only struggling into life, we might think with regret that it had not had time to become known, or to dissipate by its wisdom the perils surrounding it, and that examples were still necessary, and the severities of to-day only the forerunners of peace tomorrow. But if the government has been long enough established, if legal means and leisure have not faded in their influence, if it has been able to show itself wise, and become strong by its harmony with the public, then conspiracies cannot spring up again, nor punishments recommence, without society immediately repelling from itself both the necessity and the blame. Then power is again invested with this personal and isolated character which destroys it: it is no longer social power; and society, instead of seeing its own reflection, beholds only an interest which is not its own, wants which it disavows, and intentions in which it has no share. The justice of such a government is not true justice, and its necessities are not real necessities.

There is, in fact, in political chastisements, as in other things, a true justice and necessity, often distinct from legal justice and the necessities of power. Governments have long given up troubling themselves on the subject. In barbarous times—and their duration was long—legal justice did not seem to have been required at all; the personal necessities of power being sufficient. When attacked, it had every right to defend itself, and the execution of a conspirator called for little more delay or formality than the death of an enemy. By degrees, however, legal justice was introduced into public policy, the people began to think, and power was forced to admit that there were other things besides war, and that against crimes of this nature, as of every other, laws, forms, proofs, and judgments were necessary. This was an immense progress, and it is now approaching its consummation. But the career of progress is not yet stayed—the public cry is still, Go on! The laws which regulate the chastisement of political crimes may be insufficient or even bad; and the necessities which deliver up culprits to the laws may be false.

Society goes the length of supposing this more especially when the question is of capital punishment. Suspecting that power is isolated from it, and looks to its own interest alone, it is at the same time convinced that that interest does not suffice to legitimise punishments, and that power has not the right of defending itself at all risks. Sufficiently enlightened to know that infallible justice does not belong to any law, and that were laws even without fault in themselves, the faults of men would corrupt them in their administration, society now neither relies upon the personal wants of power nor upon the legality of its processes. It would have these wants founded on reason, and these processes in equity. Whether it obtains this or not, its demands continue; for it is aware of the justice of the debt, and though refused, it is not forgotten. Moreover, has not one political condemnation, legally pronounced, succeeded better in our days in convincing the people of its necessity and justice, than the most arbitrary executions of former times? Let not power mistake this new exaction of the public; for it is a powerful and irrevocable one, and is allied to all the progress, and all the moral wants of civilisation and of the human mind. Let it not flatter itself in thinking to escape by taking refuge behind the laws: it has long rejected their yoke, and now it would make them a shield when beaten on an open field, and would possess itself of the citadels armed against it, and then think itself inviolate. But it will be pursued to this asylum, which will be shown to have been profaned more than once by deceit and iniquity. It may plead that the punishment was legal; but it will be asked if it was just or necessary. Is it, indeed, so politically? And in what case, and under what conditions? We must descend to these questions, for the public thought itself descends to them, and will have an answer. A government which would give itself no concern in such questions, but say with Pilate—'I wash my hands of the blood of this man: see ye to it,' such governments would soon learn that they do not escape; that no deceit, no laws, can save from impending danger a power at once egotistical and hypocritical, which, in separating itself from society and truth, makes for itself a justice which is not true justice, and a necessity which is not the necessity of the country.

6

JUSTICE.

Need I say that if there were a justice anterior and superior to legal justice, there would be no legal justice. Montesquieu has made this principal truth the principal idea of his book: 'To say that there is nothing just or unjust but what positive laws order or forbid, is to say that rays were not regular before the circle had been traced.' It would be strange if natural justice, in virtue of which legal justice exists, should cease to be from the moment the latter was written. But it does not cease to be, or even to speak; it has in principle its general conditions, and on each occasion its particular will, which legal justice is bound to carry out.

I shall mention presently the progress of a struggle between the two; but we must first inquire what true justice is, before supposing it to fail in obtaining what it desires. Morally speaking, there are two parts in every action—the morality of the act itself, and the morality of the agent. The morality of the act depends on its conformity with the eternal laws of truth, reason, and morality, which no man knows fully, but only aspires to know, judging according to the degree of that knowledge of the merits or demerits of human actions. The morality of the agent resides in the intention—that is to say, in the idea which he has himself conceived of the morality of the action—and in the purity of the motives which carry him on to its accomplishment. When these two are at variance, the fact is shown in the daily conduct and common language of men. 'He has done ill,' they say, 'but he intended to do well;' that is, the action may be absolutely culpable, and yet the agent personally innocent.

But will Divine justice consider only the intention? or will it punish error? I dare not decide. Error is often caused by vanity, passion, the preoccupations of personal interest, or of pride—that is to say, by what is wrong. How does this wrong affect individual unconsciousness of error? It is seldom given to men to decide the point; God alone can see clearly into the depths of the conscience. But this is certain, that the judgment of man can neither absolve the guilt of the action because of the intention of the agent, nor condemn the agent without taking the intention into account. Thus our nature wills it.

Unable to solve such a problem, legal justice is obliged to act as if it did not exist. It declares certain actions to be culpable, and punishes those who commit them, without troubling itself to inquire whether they are guilty in intention or not. And in this there is no reproach to be cast on legal justice; for the effects of bad actions are in themselves so fatal to society, that it cannot give up to individual opinion the right of deciding upon them: it declares their nature, and takes care that its laws are observed.

But there are here two remarks to be made. First, that society thus absolutely incriminating certain actions, is bound to be in the right in its condemnations; and second, that although the laws cannot be rendered subordinate to the intention of individuals, they cannot abolish this element of man's judgment; and when, therefore, in their application they have the misfortune to punish an intention evidently pure, the natural sentiment of justice is offended. Legal justice, then, runs a double risk—that of erring in its general incriminations; and that of encountering, in the application of its rules, particular facts in which a circumstance occurs it has not taken into account, and which, nevertheless, will act powerfully upon the mind of man—honesty of intention. If there is a species of action in which this double obstacle in the way of legal justice is most real and apparent, certainly it is political crime. I have already said that the character of such an offence is variable and even conditional, and that, moreover, it is difficult to decide upon and appreciate it justly. Who does not know, too, that error is nowhere more easy, and that the purest intentions are here often associated with the most immoral acts! Some persons, struck with these facts, have gone so far as to think that, morally speaking, there are no political offences; that force alone creates them; and that good or bad fortune is the test of their culpability. I do not share in this idea in any degree. It germinates in those unfortunate times when the duties and rights of citizens disappear, or become obscured, so to speak, under the mantle of despotism, or in the storm of revolutions; but the light has not ceased to be because an eclipse has hidden it. The endeavour to change the established government, even if it did not involve any private crime, may unite in the highest degree the two general characters of crime—the immorality of the act, and the wickedness of the intention. It matters little, then, that its end is political; it does not less constitute a true crime, which ought to be punished, and perhaps with justice. Neither insurrections nor conspiracies have the privilege of innocence; and if virtue has often succumbed in its resistance to tyranny, history has no want of criminal conspirators.

What is certain is, that on no occasion is legal justice more exposed to deviate from natural justice, or has more difficulty in identifying itself with it. I leave out of question, as may be seen, everything that corrupts legal justice itself; I do not avail myself of the passions either of power, or of the judges, nor of the facility offered of twisting the laws, nor of the obstacles which the defence of the accused may meet with, notwithstanding the strict observation of forms.

Suppose impartiality and liberty everywhere, and yet I say, or rather see, that even then, and through the nature of things, true justice is in danger. The moral merit or demerit of such an action has not that degree of certainty which belongs to private crime: it depends upon an infinity of circumstances, which the foresight of the law cannot reach. The consideration of intention has more power here than anywhere else; for doubt is more easy, motives less directly personal, the causes of illusion more pressing, and the passions perhaps less impure. What will prevent these facts, for they are facts, from acting upon the public mind? Who will hinder it from seeing and taking account of them? The more difficulty the judges have in adapting the laws, the more the citizens, who judge also, will be shocked to see the laws indifferent to reasons which influence their own judgment. The imperfection of legal justice will declare itself in all its extent; and, in fact, what is the imperfection of justice but injustice?

This is felt: power has not been slow in comprehending that, in placing itself thus upon moral ground, in considering actions in their communication with the laws of eternal morality and the intentions of their authors, it would often have great difficulty in defending and proving the legitimacy of its decisions. The attempt has been made to cheat the instinct of men, to elude their disposition, to compare legal with natural justice, and in order to succeed in this, the question has been carried elsewhere. Power has taken up its ground in the social interests and the maintenance of order; it has represented crimes as hurtful rather than culpable; and shunning the absolute justice of punishments, it occupies itself with their utility.

I might say much upon this transposition of the question, but I must hasten towards my end, and shall do nothing more than indicate the error. It is not true that crimes are punished especially as hurtful, nor that the ruling consideration of punishment is its utility. Attempt to condemn and punish as hurtful an act which every one considers innocent, and you will see how much you will revolt the minds of men. Men often believe acts culpable, and punish them as such, when they are not so; but they cannot endure the sight of chastisements descending from a human hand upon actions which they think innocent. Providence alone has the right of treating innocence severely without accounting for its motives. This astonishes and troubles the human mind, which, knowing that it cannot fathom the mystery here, seeks beyond our world for an explanation. But on the earth, and where human beings are the actors, chastisement has no right but over crime. No public or private interest can induce a society, however disorderly, to believe that where there is no crime, the law may still punish to prevent a danger.

Moral offence is, then, the fundamental condition of chastisement. Human justice exacts this imperiously before it admits the legitimacy of punishment; and legal justice deceives, when, to free itself from the exigencies of natural justice, it attributes to itself another principle, and another end, and pretends to find them in utility. But it cannot thus escape from its name, which is justice, and become merely a combination, more or less skilful, of means of defence for the profit of such or such an interest. They confine the madman who has taken life, but do not punish him; because, being incapable of reason and responsibility, he is incapable of crime. Let the penal laws, then, not hope to escape, under the pretext of social interest, from being obliged to conform to the rules of natural justice: they will always have to submit to this criterion, whether in their generality or application; and when power judges and punishes, it can neither change the conditions with which the judgments of moral justice are formed, nor deviate from them without causing a universal feeling of the iniquity. That being understood, and legal justice thus brought back to the empire of natural justice, I will admit that social interest is also one of the motives which enter into the discrimination of offences and their punishment. It is not the first, for it would be without value were it not preceded by the moral reality of the offence; but it is the second, for society has the right of condemning and punishing whatever is at once culpable, hurtful, and of a nature to be repressed by the laws. Moral criminality, social dangers, and penal efficacy, are the three conditions of criminal justice, the three characters which ought to be met with in the actions it condemns and the punishments it inflicts.

That is the true ground on which legal justice is established. It participates in our greatness and our misery. It is in relation at once with the sublime nature of man and the infirmity of his condition. It cannot be pure moral justice; but it is obliged to retain its principal characteristic of punishing those only who morally deserve punishment. On this condition it undertakes to repress everything that is hurtful to society; and in this design of which an interest, or, if you please, a terrestrial necessity, is the principle, it meets with another limit, and submits to another condition—that of the efficacy of the means it uses to prevent the evils it fears—or, in other words, the efficacy of written laws and external chastisements.

I arrive now at the question, thus reduced to its true elements, and examine what is, with regard to political crimes, true legal justice, and more especially with regard to capital punishment.

Let me remark, in the first place, that of the two constituent characters of every offence—the immorality of the act, and the social danger—the more the latter predominates over the former, the more the legitimacy of capital punishment becomes doubtful, and its application cruel. There are some crimes so evident, and so odious, that the instinctive feeling of men calls for the death of the culprits as the only chastisement proportioned to the deed. But a single glance will show that these are not the crimes which can put society in great danger. They outrage natural feelings and moral laws, and show in the criminal a degree of perversity or ferocity which our nature hates to look upon, as if it were insupportable to find to what a point of depravity and dishonour it could attain. Social danger is a complex idea, the fruit of reflection and knowledge, which does not awaken in mankind this spontaneous and violent antipathy. If, in all offences, the two principles of criminality were equally and exactly balanced, the penal laws would have but little trouble. But this is not the case; for offences are, so to speak, diversely composed: in one it is immorality which predominates, in another danger; and according to the relations of these two elements of crime, the punishment must vary, not only for the sake of justice, but because the public feeling expects it, and will not see justice in the punishment on any other condition. But capital punishment being the gravest of all punishments, and much the more so now when human life is more generally respected, it is naturally adapted only to crimes of such wickedness as would perhaps provoke its infliction even if it were banished from the laws. Wherever social peril is the principal element of the offence, capital punishment is no longer founded upon our moral nature; it is excessive both in justice and in public opinion.

Every one admits that, generally speaking, political crimes are in this position. They may be detestable, but, in general, they are dangerous; and it is in this latter character that the law punishes them with severity. Let me inquire if capital punishment is a necessary, or even useful severity. It is with justice I occupy myself at this moment. But it is not in the power of any law to contrive that, in the opinion of men, the justice of a punishment should be estimated chiefly according to the moral gravity of the offence; and this measure of justice is the more natural, that the punishment strikes most severely in the person of the culprit who submits to it. The justice which deals death because of social peril, when the moral criminality is feeble or doubtful, carries injustice in the face of it; and if it happened, as it sometimes does happen in political affairs, that the intention of the accused was pure, or at least excusable—that he was mistaken in the moral character of his action, and that his error proceeded from disinterested illusions—then capital punishment would assume at once the appearance of iniquity. It would be no longer a chastisement, but the sacrifice of a human victim to terrestrial and mortal gods.

Formerly it had its excuse, I will not say in the violence of political passions, for this violence is, and will be still greater, but in their personality. Political struggles, like war, were formerly struggles, man to man, between rivals pretty nearly equal, and life was bound to the fate of power. Capital punishment, then, appeared as a species of law of retaliation, analogous not only to the state of ideas, but of realities. Danger was as near and personal as in battle. This is so true, that the greater part of the laws of barbarism—so minute in matters of private crime, so attentive in regulating the retribution according to the nature and amount of the offence—make no mention of capital punishment for a political cause. Justice had no pretence for entering here: it was of war the question was, and the danger was so visible and pressing, that the right of retaliation was too obvious to require to be written in the laws. Later, it was written, and even subjected to certain forms; but it was still retaliation, for political crimes never menaced power without first menacing the lives of men, and political perils were always preceded by personal ones. Power had thus all the rights of personal defence; but at present, the conditions of peril, as of power, are changed. The king of France has no longer enemies in the neighbouring chateaux waiting in ambush to seize his person, imprison, and perhaps kill him, and that even without the hope of reigning in his place, but merely from avarice, from vengeance, for the recovery of a domain, or for a right which he disputed, or had ravished from them. The greater number of conspiracies are vague, and a thousand barriers rise up between a government and its enemies. Instead of an individual and certain danger, the question is commonly of a complicated and social danger, formed of confused projects and means of action frequently ridiculous. How can it be thought that crimes of this kind call for capital punishment as clearly or loudly as they formerly did? Such culprits, when preparing the crime, placed themselves, as it were, at the foot of the scaffold erected by their own hands. Now this scaffold is raised laboriously, and the culprits must almost always be dragged to it from a distance, and made to mount before the eyes of a public who have seen neither distantly nor at hand either the crime or the danger. I do not believe that the condition of power is worse than it was; but if it is better, it is not power alone that should profit by the favourable change, but likewise justice. Now, justice very rarely authorises the employment of capital punishment against those crimes in which there is more appearance of social danger than moral wickedness. What will be the case if we sound the peril itself deeply? This is the motive of the punishment, the fundamental element of the criminality; and this element should at least be powerful, and the motive have the extent and reality which are attributed to it.

I will presently enter in a direct manner into this question; and I will therefore remark upon it here only in passing, and with regard to its effect on the justice of capital punishment. Observe, the question is of a social danger. I myself think with the laws. When public order is menaced, and the general forms of government or the persons who represent them are attacked, it is society which is in danger. A government must be bad, indeed, and no one can say *how* bad, before society prefers the terrible chance of distraction to even the slightest hope of reform. There are doings and secrets hidden by Providence under a veil which it alone can raise.

This admitted, I still insist and repeat that the question is of social danger. In order that society may suppose the peril to justify capital punishment, that peril must be its own, and in the danger of power it must see its own danger. However wearisome the words may have become, it is still necessary to repeat, that power exists only for society, and that all its rights correspond with its mission.

But is it quite certain that society is really so often in danger as power believes it to be? Is it quite certain that the dangers which power dreads are indeed those which it is the object of the penal laws to prevent? Is it not possible that they are neither so great, nor perhaps at all the same, as those which have appeared serious and frequent enough between power and society to render death a legiti-mate punishment?

I affirm nothing, for nothing can here be affirmed generally and beforehand; but I consider that danger in its special nature is the principal element of criminality, and I recognise in it a double char-acter. It is not certain that it does exist, nor that it is really the social danger against which the laws are directed.

The same differences which separate political from private crimes in their relations with morality, distinguish them still in their relations with the public interest. That assassination and theft are always equally hurtful to society, and morally culpable, is never doubted, and remains true whatever may be the faults or merits of the government. There is no relation between the conduct of power and the danger occurring to society from crimes of this kind. Under a tyranny, as under the most liberal regime, the same danger exists in all its extent and intensity.

In the case of political crimes, on the contrary, danger—I mean social danger—varies according to the conduct of power, and the advantages derived from it by society. Certainly, in 1802, France was in more danger from the fall of Bonaparte than in 1814; for in 1802 Bonaparte served France faithfully, both at home and abroad, while in 1814 he compromised and oppressed her. I attach no value to a permanent and blind hostility to power; but power in its turn has no right to pretend that it will be always found equally good and equally necessary, and that its dangers are always alike dangerous to society.

Thus in the very nature of that social danger, in the name of which they would take life, there is one cause of uncertainty. Here is a second cause. In private crimes, as I have already said, at the same time that the wicked and hurtful character of the offence is indubitable, its reality is certain. A murder or robbery has been committed, and a search is made for the criminal. It is certain that an offence has been committed against morality, and society put in danger, and upon whom will the punishment fall? In a political matter, the reality even of the crime is, as we have seen, often called in question; and the social danger is likewise a matter of dispute. There are men accused of conspiracy, and in order to their conviction, it must be proved that there has been a conspiracy, or, in other words, that society has been put in danger; and if the conspiracy is not proved, neither will the danger be so, at least in the eyes of the law. While in other cases the wickedness, danger, and reality of the crime are positive data, from which the accusation sets out, here the accusation goes first, and may be proceeded upon without there being a legal crime, a social peril, or a wicked act at all.

I proceed always, and it is impossible to do otherwise, upon the hypothesis, that the danger of society and that of power is one and the same. It is the only legitimate and the only legal hypothesis. It is fully established when the power is good; and it is long before it can become so bad that society may reasonably desire its fall; and in the immense interval which separates these two terms of its career, it is not to be doubted that power has a right to make use, for its own preservation, of the laws instituted for preserving the public order in its own person. But if power forfeits this right only through greater crimes, or more absurd errors, its faults before this fatal epoch do not cease to have an influence; they have the infallible effect of weakening the feeling of society as to the danger of power and its own, and thus they introduce into legal justice, especially when severe, a measure, or at least an appearance, of iniquity. When governments separate themselves from society, and feel society retiring from them, they flatter themselves they can bring it back by severity against its enemies. They are mistaken. Society judges of the severity by the opinion it has of its own danger, not by that which it forms of theirs. If only moderate punishments wore employed, it would perhaps consider them equitable; for, though discontented with power, society does not desire its destruction, or think that it has lost every right of using the laws in its defence. But if government makes use of the laws, as if society were in full harmony with it, it awakens and fortifies the feeling of disagreement, deepens the abyss which already separates them, and allows the time to pass for filling it up by other means.

Such are the conditions to which legal justice is subjected in political affairs; such are the facts in the midst of which it works, without power to escape from their bondage. It has to do with crimes whose moral perversity is sometimes equivocal, in which the intention may be excusable, and which cause more danger than aversion. It must rather consider, therefore, the danger than the immorality, and desire the prevention of perils which are not always equal or certain, nor perhaps menace alike power and society—thus causing society to doubt the equity of punishments, and giving power an air of egotism and isolation fatal, especially in our days, to its strength. When legal justice is called upon to pronounce judgment on such offences, it finds itself before a natural justice which takes account of every thought, weighs every fact, and speaks so loudly, that it must be faithfully obeyed. What is in such circumstances the character of capital punishment? Everything that could otherwise confer upon it a certain degree of legitimacy fails to do so here, not only in the eyes of attentive reason, but of the spontaneous instinct of men; and at the same time it meets with everything that can make it unjust, suspected, and odious; it is directed against danger and crime, but without the assurance of striking at a legitimate danger or the true criminal; and in order to arrive at justice, it runs a thousand chances of committing iniquity. And let not power aver that these chances are but little apparent; let it not flatter itself that the public is not aware of them, and show itself, in dealing justice, less exigent than truth demands. The public knows much of its own rights, and of the rights of true justice; and what it is still ignorant of, it will be taught. All such questions will be brought forward and debated over and over again. Men will learn to understand them, and they will insist upon the rights they discover themselves to possess. Truth will be aided in its entrance into their minds by their interests, sentiments, and even passions; and in proportion as it gains ground, capital punishment, flying before justice, will be driven for refuge to the last asylum where it can defend itself—the necessities, if not of society, at least of power—and thither we must follow it.

7

NECESSITY.

I might dispense with this part of the question. If capital punishment is of little efficacy, and I think I have proved the fact, how can it be necessary? However, I will glance at the question, even at the risk of meeting by the way the indirect paths which have conducted me to it.

Let it not be forgotten that I do not propose the legal abolition of capital punishment. Were I to demand this, it would be properly answered, that the existence of such punishments is necessary, though their application may seldom be so; and I would then have to demonstrate that not only is there no need of the punishment of death, but that it is absolutely useless to have it written in the laws. I admit that these are two distinct propositions which have no dependence on each other, and with the latter I do not meddle. I do not break this arm of capital punishment in the hands of power, I merely maintain that, in general, it is wrong to use it. I examine, then, very freely what is called its necessity; for if, in general, this does not exist, it is well to know it; and if ever real, we shall do no harm.

I have shown that the efficacy of punishments varies according to times, manners, and different states of civilisation. The case is the same with their necessity, not only because they are only necessary when efficacious, but for more direct reasons. Formerly the public strength was small, and individual strength great and licentious; and the severity of punishment made up for the insufficiency of the means of power. The wisest kings of the old ages directed frightful laws against the slightest disturbances. Were they wrong in so doing? I think not. Physical order was everywhere met by enemies capable of destroying it, and always ready to attempt its destruction. Central power, without administration, without police, stripped even of the chief rights of sovereignty, and reduced to the personal resources of the sovereign, could not defend society, or even itself, without constantly opposing physical force to physical force; and very frequently the cruelty of the laws, and the number of punishments, proved only its wisdom and desire to protect the public. The chronicles of these times, too, especially praise as just and popular those princes who punished severely and frequently. They were, like the first heroes of Greece, occupied in purging society of its bandits and monsters.

But what would society of the present day think of a power which, to maintain order, had recourse to such means? It would consider such a power as odious and insane; and this because the means of order have changed with the social constitution. On the one hand, order is maintained, as it were, of itself by the general regularity of manners, the universality of labour, and the public knowledge of the true social interests; on the other, society is concentrated: the public strength is immense, and individual strength small and little aggressive. Every physical resource and every moral influence are placed in the hands of power: it disposes of the riches of the country, of its magistrates, and of its soldiers: no one is too great or too obscure not to fear it. It is everywhere, and everywhere ready to prevent crime or danger. What is the great merit of this new condition?—The maintenance of order at the expense of little blood. When disorder has been great and general, it was not the effusion of blood which could stop it: it was by good administration, not by punishments, that Bonaparte established order in France. Five hundred years earlier, and after crises much less important than revolution, they bordered the roads with gibbets, and often without success.

That which is true of the necessities of social order is also true, and even more so, of the necessities of political order. Power can now defend itself at the cost of much less blood than society.

But let us take a nearer view of the varied characters of the old and present perils of power. Whence formerly proceeded the dangers of a sovereign, or even of a minister? From his rivals and competitors. The House of York disputes the crown with the House of Lancaster, and if one of the two exterminate the other, it will reign in safety. Charles VII. had a favourite, Giac, whom the Constable of Richmond carries oft', judges summarily, and puts to death; and then the constable returns to exercise a dominion over the king, which he has assured to himself by the assassination. Cardinal Richelieu struggles against dangers of the same kind, and defends himself by analogous means. Those who menace men in the possession of power are those who desire its possession. Political questions almost always occur between individuals; and death, which has power to decide either way, is called a necessity.

Where, now, are these enmities, and this personal ambition, which power thus disputed? Who flatters himself with seizing or preserving supremacy by the mere destruction of an enemy? No one. I do not speak of ministers: factions are not always mad; but none is so much so as to think that their chiefs may be invested with the ministry, by killing those of the opposite faction. As for sovereigns, more than one in Europe believes himself menaced; but is it by a rival or a pretender? Have the revolutions of Spain, Portugal, Naples, Piedmont, been the fruit of a litigation for the throne, the work of an ambitious subject?

It is evidently not so. The nature of political dangers is changed. The struggle is no longer between men, but between systems of government. The fate of ministers, or even that of dynasties, is not regulated by the fate of their adversaries, but by that of the system they adopt or represent. Formerly communities had masters, between whom the battle was fought; but now they are really free, for it is from them alone, or the great parties which divide them, that power can draw not merely its strength, but its pretensions. From them, also, can its dangers alone arise. The question is no longer who governs, but how he governs? Individuals are no longer,

I repeat, but the instruments and interpreters of the general interest. Is it not clear that against such dangers, and against such adversaries, capital punishment is neither powerful nor necessary?

It has, however, one effect; and it is this: at the same time that it cannot destroy those whom power wishes to destroy, it alarms those whom it does not wish to alarm. Its blows have at once less force and more extent than is necessary. The man it reaches is nothing in himself; he is feared and destroyed only on account of his connection with certain interests and general sentiments wherein the danger really resides. They desired to dissipate the danger, and have crushed only a man; and yet the stroke is felt throughout the whole sphere of interests of which his was the organ. These interests do not die with his death, nor are they even sensibly weakened; but the survivors estimate the intention which has killed him; and say that if it were possible they also would be killed—which, however, they know is not possible. And this persuasion is not only spread throughout the interests which exactly correspond with the conduct and language of the victim, but also throughout those connected with him by more distant relations, little felt, perhaps, during his life, but now compromised and menaced by his death. Thus power, by being mistaken in the nature of its dangers and enemies, brings upon itself an immense evil without obtaining the good it sought. It is doubly deceived in the importance it attaches to a man; considering him both greater and more insignificant than he really is. It has forgotten that, in ceasing to be the strength of his party, he has become its symbol; and that what he represents can no more be abolished in his person, than his person can be touched without its being felt throughout the vast circle of which he forms a part.

In this, again, the employment of capital punishment is a perilous anachronism. It is addressed to other times, other force, other dangers. It does not obtain what it promises, and it produces what is not wanted. It troubles or irritates the mass of society, to prevent the irritation and trouble occasioned by the voice or presence of an individual.

And is it now necessary against this mass itself? That would be a pity; for it would be all the more difficult to direct, and I have shown how doubtful its moral efficacy is, and that its physical efficacy is impossible. Nevertheless, if the necessity spoken of has any reality, it must be there, for the danger is there as well as the question. The possession of power is no longer the object of private struggles, once sustained by such bloody means; but the system and conduct of power are debated between it and society; and the former has indeed great need of defence, for it is vigorously attacked.

Why is it so, or rather with what intention is it so? This is the grand question. The rivals who formerly disputed the empire could not all possess it; and they were therefore obliged to kill each other. Is it a combat of the same nature which now takes place between power and society, or those great portions of society which it considers enemies? Is there that radical incompatibility, that impossibility of co-existing, which there is between two individuals who both pretend to the same place or the same property!

This is not, and cannot be. What its adversaries demand of power, is not the position it occupies, but a course of conduct which suits their views. General interests never govern in person, but desire to be governed according to their own feelings and desire. And this desire, morally speaking, the established government can always accomplish. If it will not do so, or does not know that such is in its power, the incapability may arise, though it is not in the things themselves: it is power which has created it, and the vexatious necessities thus created are its own fault.

Once set out in the way where it meets with such difficulties, can it turn back? Or if it persists, and proceeds in employing the means which those necessities command, will it succeed in its design? I affirm boldly that it will fail. In our day, every government which, through its misdeeds, draws a line of distinction between its own necessities and the social necessities is lost. The most terrible use of capital punishment cannot save it, for it can never take lives enough. We have seen situations of this kind: Bonaparte imposed upon himself the indefinite necessity for war, just as the Convention did the indefinite necessity for death: the Convention killed many, and Bonaparte vanquished many; but the time came when both the scaffold and victory refused to serve their former masters. Social necessities, repressed for a time, regained their dominion; and the power which had disowned them saw itself incapable of supporting the factitious necessities which it had put in the place of truth.

I do not admit the natural necessity of capital punishment. Or if I do, for the sake of argument, it will be only to show that the admission would avail nothing. I do not suppose that any power ever existed which took no trouble to insure its definitive success, and aspired no higher than the postponement of its ruin. In fact such power does not exist; for if a government found its ruin certain at the end of the course it followed, it would immediately leave that course: what it hoped from it was really safety. But if it were so egotistical and careless as to look no farther than the present, I would again counsel it to beware. It might formerly indulge in this indifference, and count upon a long sufferance; but now everything goes quickly, the more so that society is calm, and exhibits few tokens by its agitations of the immense strength it can wield when necessary. The approach of the Revolution did not escape the inert foresight of Louis XV. If new revolutions were still nearer, perhaps they would be still less felt under the steps of power. It would do wrong, then, to be satisfied with precautions when the time would be so short and the means so uncertain.

When we inquire on all sides into the necessities and dangers of power, from not one quarter comes the answer that capital punishment is called for by necessity, or can lessen or dissipate danger. I have considered it in all its bearings and effects; and I have almost always found it without legitimate motives; without virtue when it has, if not legitimate, at least real motives; seldom efficacious; and still seldomer just. What remains, then, but the memory of its old services! Revolutions make successful use of it, it is said, and will do so still. I know it; but revolutions are not permanent; and do governments think themselves of a like transitory nature? Prodigious error! Governments would imitate them in displaying the same strength and attaining the same results. But they forget that it is their business to lay at least the foundations of that permanence which it is the fate of revolutions to destroy, and to perish in destroying. But after all, the mistake is not surprising; for it is in our day, and perhaps for the first time, that this difference has clearly appeared. Up to the middle of the seventeenth century, revolution was, if not the permanent, at least the habitual state of European society. Delivered up to force and to rival forces, and to rivalries which were really wars, society knew neither the conditions nor the means of stability and order. The same ignorance in this respect possessed government, factions, and people. They all in their respective fortunes made use of the same arms, fell into the same practices, and produced the same results. Society has now more ambition. In tyranny or disorder it demands of government quite another thing than mere change of name. It knows what it ought to have, and what it can to do.

When the physical world came out of chaos, it still had its crises; but it also had its regularity, its repose, and its preserving laws. Though slower in emerging from disorder, the social world, the world of man, has begun to comprehend the profound difference between a state of peace and a state of war, between order and disorder, between revolutionary and regular governments. Forces differ as well as ideas, the means as well as the end. I admit that capital punishment is of use in revolutionary policy; but it is so in no other. A regular government making it a necessity, and employing its aid in laying the foundations of its repose and duration, would place itself in the path of revolution. If it proceeded only half-way, that which made the strength of revolutions would be its weakness; and if it entered fully, while changing its character it would change its destiny, and devote itself to the destruction which is the fate even of successful revolutions. Politically, capital punishment must in the present day be either a rapid succession of bloody oblations to the insatiable divinities, or a useless sacrifice to impotent idols.

Power itself, I repeat, feels this; its confidence in such means is rather a prejudice than a belief, and, like all prejudices, occasions disquiet and hesitation even at the moment of action. It, however, persists in this means; and we must state the true cause, stripping it of its pretexts and delusions, and show to which divinity the oblation belongs. This cause is neither justice nor necessity—it is fear; and not that legitimate and prudent fear which looks danger in the face, and takes means to avert it, but the blind cowardice which desires rather to be saved from itself than from the peril, and which, without rational intention or preconcerted design, adopts by chance whatever presents a hope of escape. Prudence desires safety; but fear dreads the aspect of the danger, the reality of which may perhaps be greater to-morrow. But this matters little; power will have shaken off in a moment the anxieties of its situation, and will be persuaded that it has no fear. This intractable passion never changes its nature; what it is in the obscure incidents of private life, it is still in the bosom of greatness, always more occupied with the torment than the danger; always giving itself up to vain and unreasonable expedients, if they only offer a little shelter or a little respite. And when the fears of faction are joined to the fears of power, when this blind sentiment, penetrating the mass of a party, becomes a collective passion, and pushes forward one upon another individuals who fancy themselves without personal responsibility, then reason is at an end, every calculation disappears, and there is no longer a question of necessity, utility, or justice. Fear becomes its own necessity; one of those fatal necessities the empire of which endures the more it fails in success, and into which men fling themselves both mechanically and passionately, without being in a state to reflect. A terrible example of this was given by the Convention and the Jacobins.

But fear itself is deceived, and this new and last advocate of capital punishment sees itself every moment cajoled by the hopes which attach it to the cause. Such is the power of facts, even when misunderstood and violated, that in our day political severities can no more dissipate fear than danger. Their inutility is seen even by the blindest fear; they can neither procure for power, nor for the terrified factions which make use of them, more than a momentary lull, itself a source of new anxieties. Let parties especially take heed that their condition is not less changed than that of governments. Formerly many individuals retained their strength and importance after the defeat of their party; they preserved in their original force the guarantees against reaction, and still negotiated on their own account on fair conditions. But now what are ministers when their power has left them? What becomes of the most considerable men of a party when that party is overcome! They are lost in the mass of citizens, which the public laws and true justice alone protect; they may no longer act for themselves, and have no other defenders than those principles which are obstacles to every useless severity, and every pretended necessity, and which, in the matter of punishments, interdicts to power everything with which society can dispense. It is then now more than ever the interest of all, of parties as well as of power, of individuals as well as of parties, that these principles should be recognised and introduced into the practice of government. I will try to point out the means.

8

MEANS.

s there any one who does not demand the legal abolition of
capital punishment as a political engine? I think there is, and I
have contracted the obligation of proving the fact. I might, as
is often done, have raised my voice against the severities of our
penal code; I might especially have said that, drawn up on the issue
of a violent crisis, it must bear the impress of the necessities of the
day, real perhaps at that epoch, but now false and tyrannical. Revolutions have this deplorable effect in common with barbarism, that
they bequeath to living generations the terrible laws which were
made to put a stop to their fury.

Almost everywhere in Europe the nineteenth century bears the
punishment of the disorders of the fifteenth. Revolutionary France
weighs in the same manner on constitutional France; and it will be
long before the Charter is free from the inheritance of the Empire.
But I will not pause upon this ground; ground from which power is
not easily forced, and upon which it is not always wrong in fortifying
itself. It is too often attacked by vague declamations and inconsid-
erate hopes; and declamations now-a-days are but little respected
even when their subject-matter is true. Our epoch has a predilection
for good sense; but it mistakes oddly sometimes what it honours with
this name; degrading it, and becoming itself degraded, by confer-

ring it upon aimless practices or dangerous inactivity. But even then this error may be managed; and for my part I do not ask of power that it will give us all the good laws it can, but merely that it will employ the existing laws agreeably to our interest and its own. This it can do, and sometimes does. I could easily point to laws which, though not abolished, are not, and cannot be acted upon without both shame and danger. The statutes of Great Britain are full of penal laws fallen into disuse. When their formal repeal is called for, the friends of power exclaim against it; but they would exclaim quite as much were they brought into operation.

I do not ask for repeal, which would be to forget or violate indirectly recent and positive laws. The latitude which judges enjoy in England does not belong to our tribunals; and neither is it to the tribunals that I address myself. The application of the laws is their right and duty; but the government moves in a larger and freer sphere; it has great influence in political processes, both before they come before the tribunals and after they leave them. The means I seek belong to this influence, which has them completely in its power.

The prosecution and qualification of political crimes on the one hand, and the right of pardon on the other, are the means by which government can, without changing or infringing on the laws, preserve the legal domain from capital punishment, in rendering its application more rare, and thus placing its conduct in harmony with true justice, true social necessities, true prudence and its own duty.

This liberty of action should involve reason in decision; and since the arbitrary preserves a place in the attributes of power, it should be considered to create a void that must always be filled by justice and the public good.

9

PROSECUTION AND QUALIFICATION OF POLITICAL CRIMES.

I know that the prejudiced will here rouse themselves to repel me, and I know what they will say. They pretend that everything is foreseen and absolute in the execution of criminal justice; that the administration has no more latitude than the judges, and that in the prosecution of crime it merely executes positive laws, which command and regulate its acts as well as the judgments of the tribunals. According to such reasoners, authority knows nothing of crime before the moment of prosecution; and from that moment there is no longer either will or freedom. It is bound to prosecute, for no criminal must remain unpunished; and bound to interpret the crime according to the interpretation of the law, for the legal punishment annexed to the offence must be inflicted.

Strange contradiction! Those very men who maintain such doctrines are the same who preach respect for facts and contempt for theories; and here they twist the most evident facts, in order to adapt them to the most factitious and arbitrary theory that can be conceived.

I confine myself to political crimes, of which alone I have to treat. It is not true that authority has no knowledge of these crimes, and possesses no means for their repression before the moment they come within the ken of the law. It is untrue that even then it has not the option to prosecute or not, or that, when undertaking to prosecute, it is restrained by legal texts to a single and precise interpretation.

The greater number of political crimes are conspiracies, which is proved by the numerous accusations now brought forward. But what is a conspiracy! An attempt at crime, often nothing more than the project of an attempt. The law sees crime in the project, for it requires merely the criminal intention without waiting for the commencement of the deed. In order to stay the execution of a project which has not commenced, but exists only in the common thought of its authors, authority must know what it is; it must have tracked this thought so far in the course of its formation as to be able to seize it at the moment when it is perfected in the moral course, without having made the smallest progress in the physical course. Authority, then, is not generally here, as in the case of private crimes, surprised by an unforeseen and unexpected offence, which becomes apparent only at its consummation, and leaves nothing to be thought of but the capture of its perpetrators.

On the contrary, it assists at the birth of crime, and watches it in the cradle. Why not stifle it there? What hinders it? What compels it to allow crime to grow, that it may afterwards have to prosecute it? It is surely no uncommon thing to crush a design in the bud. All wise governments have done so; they have preferred dissipating conspiracies to punishing them; and frequently, when very near their execution, they have averted the peril, and prevented the necessity of punishment, by merely showing themselves to be on their guard. Henry IV., and even Cromwell and Bonaparte, afford more than one example of this prudence. Unskilful power, and governing factions, have alone need to wait till they can arm themselves with the rigour of the laws; they alone are under the necessity of allowing crime to ripen before their eyes ere they crush it. To some the fear, and to others the passions of a party, render this perilous and culpable conduct necessary; and in our day it is of less use than ever. Two instruments now in the hands of power, and almost unknown formerly, absolve it from the necessity of having recourse to it: these are the police and publicity. By means of the police, it is enabled to penetrate into the most secret conspiracies; by publicity, conspiracies denounce and thwart themselves. Formerly authority had not so many means of obtaining information and warning; but now, besides the secret police, it has another still more efficacious agent, which, established everywhere, unveils the mysteries of society, and deprives conspirators of the resources and haunts which the general disorder offered them before. But the effect of publicity is still greater; and governments, blind as they are, lament the fact. They do not see that it works for them as well as for us; since, if publicity exposes them to the gaze of the public, it likewise exposes the public to theirs. Conspirators can no longer live in courts side by side with sovereigns, meditating on their plans by favour of the universal darkness and silence. Hypocrisy is of no more avail either for the enemies of power or for power itself. Men are formed into classes, where each takes his place according to his own sentiments or desires; treason fades before the light; every thought, every intention, is unveiled; and conspiracies, formerly the monopoly of men powerful and remarkable on the political stage, seem now reserved for the weak and obscure. The first would still conspire, if they could do so with success; but they walk in broad day; every word, every step, draws attention; whatever be their reserve and ability, they never can obtain concealment, for publicity is the condition of their importance. If they were silent, and hid themselves in secrecy, they would cease to be what they are in their party; and how can they plot successfully without silence and concealment?

Everything, in one way or other, delivers up conspiracies to power: against those of the higher class there is publicity; against those of the lower, the police; when they would be powerful, they arc difficult to form; when they would grow in the shade, they are feeble; and everywhere authority, warned in time, has a thousand means of thwarting them before they arrive at the smallest prospect of success.

How, then, can it be asserted that authority has but the severity of the law for its defence, and is therefore obliged to allow conspirators to go on towards the scaffold, tracking them quietly along that path it could so easily close! Is it imagined that punishments alone will prevent conspiracies? This is another mistake; the prospect of failure acts much more powerfully than that of chastisement in the prevention of crime. Why do so many men, in the hope of fortune or glory, face so heedlessly the cannon of battle? It is because they flatter themselves that the shot will not hit *them*. The same confidence makes in a great measure the courage of conspirators: they know very well that the law likewise deals death, but they hope to escape its cannon—that they will be under cover from the marksman—and this is the idea which accompanies and sustains them in their enterprises. But let this idea be contradicted by facts, let them see their plots penetrated and thwarted; and here will be discouragement and fear much more efficacious than the punishment of death, which they would escape if undiscovered. I do not hesitate to say that a plot baffled by the vigilance of government, even when not punished, has more effect in intimidating than the severest chastisements inflicted upon conspirators who have failed by their own fault at the moment of the outbreak.

Who will now assert that it is the legal duty of authority to allow crime to come to a head, and wait till it is before the judges, whose office it is to condemn? Who will say that it abuses its option when it stops crime and punishment in their progress towards each other? Who, on the contrary, will deny that such is its bounden duty, and a duty the more incumbent, that it has now more means of discharging, and less interest in neglecting it?

But the partisans of condemnations have yet a refuge: they say that central authority, or the higher administration, does not institute prosecutions; that the great law officers and judges of instruction have the duty as well as right of commencing of their own accord in political as in other matters; and hence they conclude that we cannot exact from a minister that which does not depend upon him, but upon numerous and independent magistrates.

If I may be permitted to say so, I entertain a profound disgust of those hypocritical arguments which, knowing their own nothingness, lie without the hope of deceiving. In my opinion this one is of the number; but yet it must receive our attention, since it is used in the controversy.

In fact I do not fear to say that, in our day, and excepting two cases within my own knowledge, no prosecutions for pure political crimes, such as conspiracies and offences of the press, have taken place but when authorised by the minister. I know well enough how these things are managed, and I do not believe that any **procureur du roi** is permitted to engage government in such processes against its will, or without its knowledge. Has this officer the right to do so, and would the ministers allow it? Is the action of the public ministry in matters of political crimes spontaneous and independent in principle? The question becomes important, and although forced to content myself with a glance, I will not elude it.

Under a constitutional regime, there are only two kinds of magistracies, responsible and irresponsible; and wherever power is established, justice and liberty demand absolutely one or other of these guarantees. It is the custom to believe that independence results either from popular election, or permanence of office; but though I believe that one of the two conditions may be necessary, I do not think it is always sufficient of itself. Independence is not so easily formed; for besides its legal, it has moral conditions, which are not obtained by an act, or in a day. It does not less depend upon the personal steadiness of the magistrate, his social position, and the idea he has himself conceived of his rights, than on the origin or duration of his functions. They might render the prefects unremovable to-morrow, but they would not be as independent as the sheriffs of England, nominated by the king, and for a single year.

I do not say this in order to deny the independence of our unremovable magistrates; for I believe that, for eight years past, and especially in the higher courts, it has made a real progress. Liberty cannot begin to dawn in a country where its spirit is not everywhere diffused, even among the depositaries of power. I do not think that this independence is yet all it should be; and it is important not to allow ourselves to be deceived by words, or to see in mere exterior signs the certainty and reality of the guarantees. However this may be, it will be admitted that if permanence of office does not secure the independence of the magistrate, his want of permanence must imply that he is responsible.

Unfortunately, responsibility is not easier to create than independence; for it likewise has more important moral conditions than those written in the laws. It has been affirmed that it flows fully and sufficiently from permanence of office. But this is not the case; for just as the world has seen perpetual magistrates very little independent, so it may see removable magistrates with a very illusive responsibility. Removableness is not in itself an efficacious guarantee, or a principle of real responsibility, but for the profit of the higher authority.

It is true that the power which can displace at its pleasure the magistrates it employs, is by that circumstance alone assured of their responsibility, so far as itself is concerned. But will that suffice? And when we speak of the responsibility which must supply the place of independence, is the question of that alone?

There is here a snare, perhaps placed without design, but into which we must not fall. Do we ask of ministers to make the responsibility of the ministry they undertake a reality? They reply that the public ministry is independent. Does it desire then to act as if it were so? They deprive it of this independence in alleging its responsibility to themselves. Thus they destroy the responsibility in alleging its independence, and the independence in the name of its responsibility.

So, when all the responsibility of a class of magistrates lies in their removableness, the higher power, to whom alone they are responsible, can alone profit by it. Surely it is not responsibility of this kind we seek, but responsibility to society itself, to justice, and the public interest; without which removableness is but a falsehood and a new danger.

How to escape this danger? How to realise the social responsibility of removable magistrates? There are but two means: the dependence which results from removableness must be combated by the elements of independence, which, giving magistrates a proper power, restricts the higher power in the exercise of its right, and imposes upon it the obligation of using it but seldom, with caution, and only in a case of absolute necessity; or the dependence must be complete, and the responsibility of magistrates concentrated entirely upon the high administration, which alone offers any hold to political responsibility, since it alone is called upon to the public discussion of its acts and their constitutional justification.

If I had to choose between these two means, the first would

appear to me to be greatly preferable. I own that I hold that responsibility to be of little value which leaves the place where it originated to seek afar off for that where it will become real, and travels from agent to agent, growing weaker from each transition, until it has found the individual with whom it must rest. It has, in my opinion, a great chance, after so many changes, of becoming in the end illusive, perhaps even unjust. And I think besides that, without giving to the public ministry the same degree of independence which belongs to the judges, we may regret that it has none at all. Magistrates reduced to the condition of simple agents are no longer magistrates. They are wanting both in authority and dignity, for dignity goes with independence. Moreover it happens, in the nature of things, that in many cases, in matters of private crimes, for instance, the action of the public ministry is truly spontaneous and free.

Hence it follows that its position becomes a false one in those cases where it has no longer spontaneousness and liberty; and the falseness of its position proves a means of deceiving the public, who are still told of the independence of these magistrates, when, in fact, as in political affairs, there is no such thing. There results from all this for the public ministry a false and bastard position, which compromises it in the ideas of the people, but which would cease if it were indeed a magistracy invested with some personal consistence, with a proper degree of strength, with independence enough to feel itself under the weight of a direct responsibility, and summoned for the service of power, though without holding from it every element of its importance, and every law of its action. I repeat, I would much prefer, and for the sake of liberty as well as of the magistrates, a public ministry thus constituted to the hierarchical subordination of the purely administrative regime; but such things are not the work of one generation nor of a legislative will. Shall we obtain them one day, and on what conditions can such a magistracy have a place in our constitutional system? I have nothing to do with this question here; but assuredly, when the guarantees of the social responsibility of the public ministry are not found to have a degree of independence accordant with its mission, we are in the right to seek them elsewhere. They may, it is true, be of a partial and haphazard nature; but no matter, it is all that remains to us. There is here a great power, a power whose action is in a great measure arbitrary; and we need a visible and real responsibility, at least for discussion. This is nothing more than a right. I again affirm that in political matters the subordination of the public ministry is complete; that here it possesses no spontaneousness; that in almost every case it is the higher administration that orders or holds back the prosecutions, and decides upon their propriety and direction. Since it does exercise this power, it is bound to make use of it reasonably, according to the public interest: it is bound to prove that it does use it thus; and it stands responsible for using it in excess, or without necessity.

Here, then, is the first road opened to the economy of capital punishment, the first means of sparing the tribunals the necessity of a frequent application of the rigours of the law. It rests with power to smother many political offences without prosecuting them. In the present state of society it will find this easy; and in the present state of the magistracy it has the absolute right, for the prosecutions are in its hand.

Let us see the cases where it is obliged, or thinks it indispensable to prosecute. It has not been able to arrest the offence before the complete development of its legal character, or at least till it supposes chastisement to be necessary. Is it from that moment so bound by the laws, as to have no influence in the direction of prosecutions—but is obliged to force the criminal on towards the scaffold whenever the crime appears susceptible of a capital qualification?

Whoever has watched for some years past the course of political processes, must have remarked two circumstances. Sometimes the judgment has not accorded with the indictment; the court of assizes has believed it a duty, in the position of the question, to lessen the severity of the public ministry, and substitute for a capital crime one of less gravity; or the public ministry itself has reduced its first pretensions, and combated even the first finding which had admitted them. This is what M. Courvoisier at Lyons did in the affair of Maillard. More frequently the public ministry is obstinate in rigorously characterising the offence, and exacting death as its punishment; and in such cases we have seen the judges and jurors acquit the accused, rather than lend themselves to such excessive severity; so that men who would have been subjected to some punishment, had the sentence demanded been moderate, are fully acquitted because it was desired to drive them to the scaffold. I could cite many instances of this kind, but I abstain from doing so, in tenderness to the innocence thus legally proclaimed.

What do these facts prove, if not the uncertainty which often accompanies the characterisation of political crimes? And in this uncertainty, what obliges power to class them under the gravest heads, and to show itself eager for capital punishment at the risk of obtaining none at all! If I am not mistaken here, and if, in political matters, justice, necessity, and efficacy are generally wanting in capital punishment, must not power be too happy in not having to grapple with so terrible an anomaly, and the perils which spring from it, but to find, in the very nature of such crimes, sufficient flexibility to make it easy to characterise them more moderately! Reason commands it, the reason of interest as well as of equity; for nothing can more compromise power than failing totally in a capital accusation; and experience has proved that, notwithstanding the weakness of our judiciary institutions, it could very well do without the blood it had refrained from demanding.

I am aware that it complains of the insufficiency of our laws, and imputes to them both the severity and the ill-success of its issues. They admit, it says, of no alternative: conspirators must either be arraigned as such, and the punishment of death invoked, or the prosecution must be abandoned; for there is nothing under this classification and punishment commensurate with the offence.

I do not admit the excuse. The penal code, in inflicting on the unsuccessful proposal to conspire the punishment of a long banishment, has opened wide a door for the classification of offences of a similar kind. Few attempts characterised as conspiracy correspond fully with the definition of the law; and since some features are wanting, the accusation must be indeed absurd, and the crime imaginary, if it could not be found an unsuccessful proposal of conspiracy. Why not reduce it, from the first, to this character? Because exile is considered too mild; because we are still under the dominion of those prejudices, and this false confidence in capital punishment which I have combated. The government thinks there is no safety but in bloodshed; and at the risk of not obtaining this blood, they seek capital condemnation, because ten years of exile are supposed to be nothing.

Ten years of exile nothing! Good God! with what enemies then do you deal? Are these men so powerful, so European, that they will carry wherever they go their fortune and their influence, that they will everywhere find a **point d'appui** from which to shake your power, and stretch forth at any distance arms long enough to reach you? That Henry III. still feared the Duke de Guise in refuge at Brussels—that Elizabeth was inquieted by Mary Stuart in France— that even in St Helena Bonaparte made his enemies tremble—may be conceived; but almost all the conspirators you prosecute are men without fame, without wealth, unknown beyond their canton, and who are unable to find in foreign countries anything but misery and oblivion. You then arm yourself even with their wretchedness; you say that it will drive them to any hazard, and that they will attempt to return and rear against you new dangers. There are indeed persons who have been sufficiently daring, who have maintained some correspondence, who have published proclamations, and who have even come to the frontiers of the country. But what risk did you run? Did M. Cuquet de Montarlot give you serious cause of alarm? Were the administration, the police, the gendarmes, the custom-houses, the passports, found to be useless against such paltry designs? And if there is really danger in any part of our frontiers, do you believe it to be caused by the presence of a few obscure and impoverished exiles?

I cannot pause upon such an idea. No, assuredly, it is not true that the punishment of exile is illusory; and if it were so, it would be from very different causes than the personal importance of the convicts. Few French men are anything in France: out of France they are nothing.

If power were in the right; if it were true that there does exist a hiatus in the penal code, and that, in desiring to inflict the severest punishments upon political crimes, our law has forgotten to define those that are susceptible of the lighter chastisements, would it be very difficult to find a remedy? It is not a rare thing to see the administration coming to the legislative power to complain of the insufficiency of the penal laws, and to ask new punishments for new offences.

In general, I know, the question in such cases is of aggravation; but if it were desired to soften the laws on account of the severity of their pretensions involving a vexatious impunity, are not the same paths open! What obliges power to remain under the necessity of requiring capital punishment for crimes which really do not merit it? What condemns it to put the judges and juries so often to the alternative of pardon or injustice? Is it not permitted to bring less violent indictments involving lighter punishments? Would it not be welcome thus to show itself at once moderate and prudent, caring alike for order and equity! It is possible that our laws in regard of political matters require some reforms of this kind, and that power, in calling for more merciful punishments, would obtain them more easily. I see nothing to prevent this new means from being adopted, of restricting the circle of capital punishment.

Thereby would be gained the important advantage of no longer offering to the country and to Europe the spectacle of such continual accusations of great political crimes brought against obscure and powerless men, and which exhibit authority always ready to arm itself with all its strength against those who are obviously incapable of putting the fate of the state in jeopardy. I do not think that power can have any profit in thus revealing all its maladies, or, if we must call them so, the maladies of the society it governs. The moral effect of such a spectacle is deplorable. It is impossible not to conclude from it, either that the revolutionary fever possesses the people, or that power is unfit to govern. That party men, delivered up to the egotism of frantic passions, delight in repeating that France is full of lepers and brigands; that general disorder is ever on the point of raging; and that the parliamentary opposition is itself but the organ of the most unsocial interests and the blindest fury—all this may be conceived: but the national honour has not been committed to the keeping of these men; they are not held in respect by their country, nor do they watch over its consideration and tranquillity in Europe. But a government must think of these duties; it belongs to the state, and it is commanded to conceal, if such exist, the moral wounds of the country, expecting meanwhile that its good conduct will succeed in curing them. Surely it is not its part to disclose such deformities, that it may avail itself of them for legitimising such or such a system of administration! I wish, however, for neither illusion nor falsehood; for I do not believe that power is bound to flatter society, or to appear ignorant of the vices or danger fermenting in its bosom.

What good can it expect from exhibiting the country so often troubled and itself so often menaced with such agitations! It is always a melancholy and dangerous situation for a government to live upon the faults and errors of its people, and to seek its strength in the manifestation of the weaknesses past or present of the country. Besides, is not power aware that disorder is contagious, especially after a great crisis, and that it is of the utmost importance to stifle its symptoms in order to remove its temptation? Much is expected from example; but it is forgotten that although there is example in punishment, there is the same in crime, and often more efficacious. Who will doubt that in a country where theft is rare, the very rarity would more powerfully contend with the temptation than would elsewhere the severest chastisements of the thieves? How can so evident an analogy be mistaken? A thousand times has it been observed: we have seen murder call forth murder, incendiaries produce incendiaries: the perverse dispositions of men reveal themselves when called upon; and when once set forth on their course, the rigour of the law must long be exercised against them before they stop. This peril is greater in political crimes than in any other; for there the guilty are more liable to self-deception, and excite in the public, by whom they are surrounded, much less contempt and aversion. What madness, then, in power to hold up those continual provocations to such crimes, which spring from the parade of political prosecutions! Truly one cannot admire too much its inconsistency. The publicity of judicial debates not only incommodes, but terrifies it; and it tries to get rid of the inconvenience by concealing its incomparable advantages. Such publicity, it tells us, reveals the temptations as well as the terrors of crime; yet it takes no care to make this spectacle rare, to refrain till the last extremity from opening a school the lessons of which it holds in such dread. How does it not see that, if these were less frequent and less solemn, they would have less power? Their solemnity depends much upon the gravity of the punishments in perspective: the public cannot feel the same interest in a process which gives but a few years of imprisonment, as if the question were of a life. If power knew how to read the souls of the audience in such a debate; if every thought, every emotion which it raises were developed before its eyes, it would itself be troubled, and would assuredly doubt whether its expected profit were not an illusion. But, blind and unsteady, it is ignorant of this: it is not aware that every proceeding, every word of the politically accused whom it urges on to the scaffold, becomes the subject of the most animated conversations and the boldest commentaries, and that the slightest particular of his fate occasions the most lively and most enduring reflections, even in men who would not themselves have committed his imputed crime, and who would have felt but little interested, if the terrible destiny which weighs upon him had not stirred up from the bottom of their hearts every element of pity and sympathy. Such is the effect of political prosecutions which lead to the punishment of death: an effect mysterious in its extent, but infallible, and which baffles in this case the hopes of power, although power knows not how much what its supposed gains have cost.

I might go much farther: consequences present themselves in crowds, and all proclaim that the commonest prudence, the merest personal interest of power, counsels it to lower the rate of its political accusations, to diminish their number, and to make use of every means at its disposal to frustrate conspiracies without prosecuting them; in fine, to employ very rarely the punishment of death—as rarely as it is attended by true justice and true necessity. Observe what an employment a wise and skilful administration might make of its influence; observe how, without disarming itself, and without interference with the laws, it might introduce into government practical reforms conformable to the actual state of society, to the instinct of morals, and to the real interests of power. It is for such purposes that it is allowed, even here, that measure of the arbitrary always inseparable from the course of human affairs. In vain it would deny that it possesses and is able to use such a faculty. Power is full of contradictions. When incommoded by the laws, it claims arbitrary authority; when responsibility weighs upon it, it pretends to be merely the executive agent. But these sophisms deceive no one; truth easily compasses them; and when political processes multiply beyond measure, and capital punishment is continually invoked, it will be power, and not the laws, that will suffer. I have shown how, either before the prosecutions or by their direction, the legal domain of punishment might be restricted. Let us now see what influence might be exercised after judgment has been passed.

10

THE PRIVILEGE OF MERCY.

I meet here with prejudices of another kind, as unreasonable in my opinion, but more respectable, inasmuch as they are probably more disinterested and sincere. Some persons suppose that the privilege of mercy is a right purely royal, with the exercise of which the ministry has nothing to do, and of which the king alone disposes, with reference to nothing more than personal clemency or equity, and without any ministerial responsibility being attached to it, or making it a part of the enginery of government. This was likewise the opinion of the Constituent Assembly; and what resulted from it? That, in the constitution of 1791, the privilege of mercy was suppressed.

That this was a great error, none is more convinced than I; but the error was consequent on the idea which still dominated in the minds of men. Under the constitutional regime, where the inviolability of the monarch is founded upon the responsibility of ministers, no power of action would belong to him, and no act could emanate from him unaccompanied by this responsibility. Whence, otherwise, could the royal inviolability derive its meaning, or, in other words, its guarantee?

The Constituent Assembly was aware of this necessity; and yet, from the influence of old habits, the privilege of mercy was still considered as a right purely personal and irresponsible in its nature. And they came to the conclusion that it should not continue.

It is now re-established, and very properly so, like many other rights of which the sudden revolution had stripped the royal power; but at the same time, like all these rights, it has reentered the dominion of the principle which is the permanent and tutelary condition of this power. The king, acting by advice, and inviolable in everything, rules under the countersign of a responsible minister. Let those who still doubt on this point at least examine it. They have already abandoned two similar opinions: they said that the right of dissolving the Chamber of Deputies, and that of creating peers, were in like manner personal to the king, free from all ministerial responsibility. But in 1816 and 1819, the king openly exercised both by the advice of his ministers. Such was the power of facts, that it became necessary to pay homage to the truth of principles, and recognise a responsibility which appeared to flow from these acts of government. The most violent, as well as the most enlightened members of the party now in power, have exclaimed against the ministry to which they imputed them; and which, I think, would no more hesitate now than it did then. The privilege of mercy is not of another nature, for it is not placed out of the constitutional pale, and perhaps occupies a position not less important. It is forming too mean an idea of it to regard it as merely intended to illustrate the goodness of the prince, and to call down blessings upon his name. It may produce this effect, and that is one of its advantages; but it is founded upon more extended causes and more general interests. In fact it is a portion of the right of justice, a remnant of the times when princes, exercising judgment themselves, could, according to circumstances, either condemn or absolve. In the progress of social order, the right of judging has departed from the prince, but he has retained the right of pardoning. What a great example of that mysterious Wisdom which presides over the development of civilisation, and which, unconsciously to man, calls forth from the bosom of facts institutions and customs conformable to those eternal truths, the laws of which human wisdom alone could never have discovered!

Balanced between the need of justice and the impossibility of giving up to the capricious or perverse will of man the right of ruling, society felt first the perils of arbitrary power; and in order to free itself, established fixed laws and independent judges, strove against the influence of individual will upon judgments, and tried to write justice beforehand, and to connect with it beforehand the judges. A great amelioration has been the result of these efforts. But truth has not allowed itself to be seized all at once; and the inevitable nature of things has not always consented to be seen in the texts of the laws. After having struggled against the arbitrary principle, it has been necessary to recur to it; and in the same way that the precision of legal judgments has been invoked against the imperfections of men, so the conscience of man has been invoked against the imperfections of the judgments. Thus the necessity of the arbitrary principle, indomitable in our weakness, makes itself felt after its danger; and in default of that infallible judge who is wanting upon earth, the freedom which the law wished to subdue in order to rule has now in its turn come to the succour of the law itself.

Such is the inevitably vicious circle of human affairs. The great error of the Constituent Assembly, both in its theories and institutions, was to mistake this fundamental element of our condition, and suppose that truth, reason, and justice could belong, fully and perfectly, to certain forms and certain powers, and that it was thus possible to banish completely the arbitrary principle: an arrogant attempt, which could only lead to tyranny. Such an attempt can never succeed, for it is in direct opposition to the present system of government which the people favour, and which it was the object of the Constituent Assembly to found. It is the grand characteristic of the representative government to accept freely, in many cases, the imperious necessity of the arbitrary principle, and at once to remedy its defects in associating it with responsibility. The greater progress we make in this system, the more shall we be convinced that responsibility in all its forms, and by the most diverse means, moral or legal, direct or indirect, is its most essential character and most powerful spring. A complete and admirable system, then, it must be, since it recognises at once the weakness of our nature and respects its dignity. In this system it is impossible to prevent arbitrary power, however needful its presence may be, from being suddenly seized upon by responsibility. If it were otherwise, the entire system would be falsified. The privilege of mercy would be no privilege at all. Has the nature of this right been well examined?

It is the right of suspending, or annihilating the law; it is that 'dispensing power' which was one of the causes of the terrible struggle of the English nation and the Stuarts. The kings of England maintained that it was their privilege to recognise in particular cases the injustice or imperfection of certain laws, and so to exempt such or such citizens from them. The country would never agree to this, and the country was right. All the laws and all the public rights would have been enervated by such a privilege. The ministerial responsibility alone could, in exercising the privilege of mercy, preserve society from that peril; for if it remains ignorant of one function of power, it will soon be so of others. The dispensing power of the Stuarts desired likewise to have the right of exempting the Catholics from certain penal clauses; but the parliament knew well that, in policy as in morals, bad principles must be put down, and it would neither allow itself to be over-ridden nor neutralised.

Where could falsehood elsewhere hide itself? Who does not know that in the exercise of the privilege of mercy, as in every other step, the king commonly decides according to the advice of his ministers, whose duty it is to study the case, and submit to him the reasons for decision? Who is ignorant that, on every occasion, the petitions for pardon are addressed to the minister of justice, and become in his office the object of an examination, which produces a report to the king, who thereupon grants or refuses his clemency? This clemency is free, absolutely free, yet it desires to be enlightened; and if I am not mistaken, when such petitions are addressed directly to the sovereign, he himself orders them to be referred to his minister, to the end that the regular course of administration should be uninterrupted. In political matters this regularity is still more scrupulous, for there the severity or clemency may affect the entire conduct of the ministry, and the general state of the country. Such affairs are always a subject of serious deliberation in the council. It matters not whether the determination which ensues be conformable or not with the advice of ministers, for if they neither disavow nor fail in carrying it into execution, it is their own; it belongs to their responsibility, like all other royal decisions, the secret of which none knows better than they. They have, then, no right to declare themselves absolved from the consequences; they have given their advice, fulfilled their task, and must be answerable. The mantle of royal inviolability is itself inviolable, and no one can pretend to cover himself with it.

Is the privilege of mercy thus brought under the common law of constitutional principles, and fixed in the province of the upper administration, an engine of government which might be used to advantage to-day, and if so, what use should be made of it as regards political crimes?

To those who would persist in seeing in it merely a means of extending mercy to individuals, and not a political instrument of general government, Montesquieu has replied for me:—'Letters of pardon,' says he, 'are a great instrument of moderate governments; the power by which a prince may pardon, when exercised with wisdom, may have admirable effects.'

And can it be otherwise? It is especially for political crimes that the privilege of mercy seems to be reserved—crimes frequently of an equivocal nature, to which sincere errors may be allied, and sentiments worthy of respect; by which society may not always appear to be threatened; in which the peril—the principal element of the crime—is wanting; and, in short, in which want of success acts more efficaciously than chastisement. In private crimes, pardon supposes error, or at least excessive severity of judgment: and it may thus have the inconvenience of shaking the authority of legal justice, or the confidence in the wisdom of the laws. Too widely used, it would point out vices to reform in the tribunals or the codes; it would make the royal clemency a new jurisdiction, a tribunal of equity called upon to revise all criminal judgments; and offering, neither in the administrative instruction which preceded the sentences, nor in their forms, any of the prudent warrants of ordinary tribunals. In political crimes, none of these inconveniences are to be dreaded: here pardon implies neither the error of the chief judges, nor even, in a legal point of view, the immoderate rigour of their decree. It neither compromises nor shakes their authority in any way: it simply reveals the intention of the sovereign of treating with gentleness even those of his subjects of whom he has to complain: a moral and politic intention, that has no dispute with the laws, and does not alter their credit, but addresses itself to a circle of sentiments or ideas completely foreign to that in which legal justice moves. One may even presume that, in such a sphere, the habit of clemency, far from discouraging the severity of jurors or judges, would make them less timid and more free. The idea is so natural, that the public has sometimes seemed to believe that a particular political condemnation had been pronounced only in the prospect of a pardon to neutralise its rigour. Thus, by an economy of blood, we might perhaps gain the facility of example; power would have all the merit of the moderation, and the citizens who, in the courts of assize, often hesitate, and with good reason, when it is necessary to condemn a man to the scaffold, would manifest with less pain their disapprobation of his attempts or his designs.

We fear the effects of impunity; we fear that confidence of courage which supposes moderation to result from weakness or cowardice. But I have never known any governments taxed with weakness but those that were really weak; and with regard to them, I know of none to whom rigour can supply the wanting strength. It is the most obstinate error of power to take on every occasion the effect for the cause. Thus, if discontent is general, it imputes it to the symptoms by which it is manifested. Since strong governments have been rigorous, it concludes that every rigorous government must be strong. I have already exposed this absurd mistake, and I find it here in all its grossness. Doubtless it is possible that mildness may be allied to weakness, and malevolence encouraged by it; but it is not from the mildness the evil comes, but from the weakness—that real weakness which betrays itself in severity the same as in mercy. I am ashamed to insist upon these commonplaces of common sense; but what is to be done? When the error is a vulgar one, it is by vulgar truths it must be subdued. Besides, what do you call impunity? Is it banishment, imprisonment, transportation? These are the next punishments to death, and you may substitute them for it. Amusing impunity! Do you not see that similar commutations are in absolute harmony with the present state of morals and the nature of political dangers? We are no longer in the time of strong and indomitable passions, which survived suffering and irons, and were found, after twenty years of impotence and captivity, in all their energy. Such sentiments belong to those epochs when even liberty is morose, when life offers few distractions and few pleasures, when the ideas which occupy the mind of man are few and simple, and are not of that conflicting nature which confuses and agitates the soul, drifting at random in the midst of an advanced civilisation. In our day the prison or banishment takes men away from a commodious and pleasant existence; and they regret a thousand enjoyments they knew not in former times, and receive from punishment much more efficacious warning. Yet they do not experience in exile or prison those ferocious violences which formerly irritated them so deeply, rendering them as much more untractable as they were more miserable. In the present day, even without liberty, a prisoner's physical sufferings are not such as to disable him from reflecting on the causes of his misfortune, recognising his imprudences or errors, calming perhaps, or at least terrifying himself, and returning one day into society more softened than enraged. A power, however wanting in skill, would find, I am sure, in these features of our social state a thousand means of working upon the condemned enemies whose lives it had spared. Besides, whose is the necessity for the blow? Political perils are not immutable; though substantial now, perhaps in two years they will have disappeared; and the man who is to-day their instrument, will then have neither the power nor even the idea of hurting the consolidated government.

A bandit or an assassin robs or kills on his own account, from motives purely personal, and without troubling himself as to whether the disposition of society is favourable, or whether he will receive from it protection or support. But political crimes are not so isolated: right or wrong, they are in correspondence with the condition of the public, from whom they promise themselves indulgence or even succour; they are to a certain extent crimes of circumstances, and would not have been committed, or perhaps conceived, if circumstances had been different. And wherefore be in such a hurry to kill when the circumstances may change! The present peril is foreseen; the condemned is in the hands of power, which, in sparing his life, may yet retain him in impotence while the danger continues. The danger past, of what use is severity? Is it so difficult to keep some mercy in reserve for days of security? If you have not this foresight, but hasten to irrecoverable steps, know you what will happen? That the trouble and danger will go on increasing, and you will be demanded an account of your needless severity. But if fortune is more favourable, and danger departs, and the storm subsides—then, when safety has returned, and society sees no more in a pressing peril the motive of your rigour, it will forget peril and motive together: it will remember only your bloodthirstyness; and governed by that instinct of truth which does not permit us to attribute to the death of a few men the return of peace and order, it will say that you have sacrificed to your fear or your vengeance those whom you might have spared without danger.

It would be right to think thus; and the fact which is revealed in this sentiment is the political uselessness of capital punishment. It must be seen from a distance, in order to be judged properly as to its effects; and more than once, governments have had to regret having lost the opportunity offered to them by the privilege of mercy. Hurried away by the passions or perils of the moment to give it full sweep, they have afterwards found themselves weighed down by obligations and recollections, the burden of which they deplored. In the midst of the mobility of human affairs, it is a great fault in power to bind itself by irrecoverable acts. A day may come when the blood which it shed, apparently forgotten, will bubble up between it and the men it has most need of. Formerly, the brutality of manners and power of personal interests were such, that obstacles like this gave way easily before new circumstances; but in the present day, notwithstanding the unchangeable levity of our nature, they are more real and more difficult to surmount, for public opinion lends them a force which they could not always derive from the constancy of individual sentiments. The prudent use of the privilege of mercy disperses them, as it were, beforehand, and leaves power a freedom of movement, which it is of great importance for it to preserve. In what consists wisdom, if not in foresight! Let governments be possessed of that, and I doubt if they will frequently make use of capital punishment.

Here is the last consideration. I have hesitated to present it, for I would not be accused of advising cowardice; and yet I will set it down—for it is true. Formerly the depositaries of power, ministers or others, risked in political struggles their life as well as position. It was the necessity of the time that such combats should always have a revolutionary character, and that no one could retire from them vanquished to find security in repose. The constitutional system and public manners have changed this gloomy condition of public men; they may now fall without danger, and even re-enter the lists for the recovery of their power. The people are better governed, and the governors more safe. May nothing alter this new aspect of political life! Ministers would deceive themselves did they think to shake off the responsibility which rests upon them by disputing its limits. When facts become serious, and the gravest interests are compromised, then subtilties lose their empire; everything is decided with simplicity, and they answer in their whole conduct for all the counsels they have given or omitted. I know that such a prospect, presenting itself to the eyes of a public man, should not induce him to relax in his duties: it should rather teach him the obligation to look well about him; not to believe lightly in pretended necessities, or to satisfy himself in the days of his power with such frivolous excuses as have no value when those days are past; to reduce as far as in him lies that circle of political death-punishment already so happily contracted; and, in short, to employ to this end, in his function of counsellor to the throne, the whole force which his responsibility lends him.

11

CONCLUSION.

Before concluding, I have read again that treatise in which it is said we may discover the deepest and most odious secrets of tyranny—the treatise of **The Prince**; and I have found a passage which I wish to quote. In its expressions, and even ideas, it belongs rather to the manners and policy of the sixteenth century than to our own; it speaks more especially of personal enmities and treasons, of assassinations and political perils which belong more to the ferocious struggles of personal ambition than to the clashing of general interests or contending systems of government.

However, it is good to know what was thought of conspiracies and their importance by a great man, who, living in the midst of punishments and factions, an unmoved observer of facts and their results, undertook to teach governments by what prudence they might surmount such casualties.

'One of the most powerful safeguards,' says Machiavel, 'that a prince can have against conspiracies, is to be neither hated nor despised by the mass. The man who conspires believes always that, by the death of the prince, he will satisfy the people; but if, on the contrary, he thinks it would offend them, he will not have the courage to go forward, for the difficulties which surround conspirators are infinite. We know by experience that there have been many conspiracies, but few that have succeeded. He who conspires cannot do so alone, nor choose his companions but among those whom he supposes to be discontented. But when you have intrusted your secret to a malcontent, you have furnished him with the means of throwing off this character, for, by revealing the design, he may hope for every kind of profit. Seeing, on the one hand, the profit certain, and on the other nothing but doubts and perils, he must be a rare friend indeed, or else a very obstinate enemy of the prince, to keep faith with you. Reducing the thing to the most simple terms, I say that, on the side of the conspirators, all is fear, mistrust, and dread of chastisement; while on that of the prince are the majesty of power and of the laws, and the strength of his friends and of the state. When to all this is joined the good-will of the public, it is impossible for any one to have the temerity to conspire. In ordinary cases, a conspirator has much to fear before the perpetration of the crime; but here he has to fear even after it; for, the crime accomplished, he will have the people for enemies, and so can hope for no refuge. A number of examples on this point might be given, but I will content myself with one which occurred in the time of our fathers. Annibal Bentivoglio, who governed Bologna, having been assassinated by the Canneschi in a conspiracy, and leaving no heir but John, who was still an infant, the people rose after the murder and massacred all the Canneschi, an effect of the popular good-will enjoyed at that time by the family of Bentivoglio. ... From this I conclude that a prince has little to fear from conspiracies, if he enjoys the good-will of the people; but that, if the people are his enemies, he has to fear everything and every citizen.'*

I would not be so confident as Machiavel, nor go so far as to say that the popularity of power is enough to discourage the audacity of conspirators. But if, in the sixteenth century, the most profound adept in Italian policy thought that the strength of power against conspiracies resided not in its punishments, but in the satisfaction of

---

*   *Il Principe*, c. xix.; Opere di Nic, Macchiavelli, t. vi. pp. 316-318.

general interests, and the relation borne to them by the system of government, how will it be in our own day? Machiavel found conspiracies very difficult to deal with, and capital punishments very insufficient when power was not popular; and now, when the question is to stir up the masses to a struggle against the powerful organisation of great governments, would conspirators have fewer obstacles to contend with? Would capital punishments have more virtue? I have already answered the question. The tasks of justice and policy are distinct, more so than they ever were, and the one cannot supply the place of the other. If policy is not equal to its own, or if it is ignorant of, or offends the public will, in vain would it summon to its assistance punishments against individuals. Punishments may destroy men, but they can neither change the interests nor sentiments of the people. But what do I wish? Neither effeminacy nor impunity. To combat a useless rigour, I have merely gathered these facts together, and have shown that against moral dangers and general forces such rigour is without efficacy. The character of generality which the dangers of power now bear will be also found in these means. It may kill one or several individuals, and severely chastise one or several conspiracies; but if it can do no more than this, it will find the same perils and the same enemies always before it. If it is able to do more, let it dispense with killing, for it has no more need of it: less terrible remedies will suffice. It will see, as Machiavel says, that a government protected by public approbation stands on a vantage-ground, where conspiracies are as impotent against power as capital punishment is impotent against conspiracies.